T0129726

The Truth
Shall Set You Free

Enoch Mamo

BALBOA.
PRESS

A DIVISION OF HAY HOUSE

NIV: THE HOLY BIBLE, NEW INTERNATIONAL VERSION®, NIV® Copyright © 1973, 1978, 1984, 2011 by Biblica, Inc.® Used by permission. All rights reserved worldwide.

Balboa Press books may be ordered through booksellers or by contacting:

Balboa Press
A Division of Hay House
1663 Liberty Drive
Bloomington, IN 47403
www.balboapress.com
1 (877) 407-4847

Because of the dynamic nature of the Internet, any web addresses or links contained in this book may have changed since publication and may no longer be valid. The views expressed in this work are solely those of the author and do not necessarily reflect the views of the publisher, and the publisher hereby disclaims any responsibility for them.

The author of this book does not dispense medical advice or prescribe the use of any technique as a form of treatment for physical, emotional, or medical problems without the advice of a physician, either directly or indirectly. The intent of the author is only to offer information of a general nature to help you in your quest for emotional and spiritual well-being. In the event you use any of the information in this book for yourself, which is your constitutional right, the author and the publisher assume no responsibility for your actions.

Any people depicted in stock imagery provided by Getty Images are models, and such images are being used for illustrative purposes only. Certain stock imagery © Getty Images.

Print information available on the last page.

ISBN: 978-1-9822-0067-1 (sc)
ISBN: 978-1-9822-0069-5 (hc)
ISBN: 978-1-9822-0068-8 (e)

Library of Congress Control Number: 2018903373

Balboa Press rev. date: 04/18/2018

Contents

Chapter 3: The Two Energies

Chapter 4: The Present Moment

Chapter 5: Fear and Worry

Chapter 6: What Is Poverty?

Chapter 7: Victim Identity

Chapter 8: Power of Belief and Faith

Chapter 9: Being Yourself and Conformity

Chapter 10: Living in the Real World

Chapter 11: What Is Not Life

Chapter 12: True Living

Chapter 13: The Illusion of Loss

Chapter 14: Anger

Introduction

This book is a result of my decision to stop reading the teachings of others in search of fulfillment, spiritual harmony, and the meaning of life and our existence. It forced me to live and interpret spirituality based on my own everyday life experience. I came to appreciate and value my intuition and accept my life with all its imperfections. I hope this book will also help you to stop the search and teach you to accept yourself and your present conditions in order to live a life full of happiness, abundance, health, and many other blessings.

The change in my attitude and perspective led me to enjoy the present moment rather than trying to achieve some state of spiritual or external fulfillment to start living a happy life. Sometimes I was stuck in a state of seeking or searching for a perfect life with a clear purpose based on external accomplishment to be achieved in the future. The search was a futile effort that wasted years of my life. I was not too sure what kind of life I was even seeking, and this made the present unpleasant and led me to endless searches in the hope of finding a perfect and enlightened future. It was a life of chasing after the wind.

I imagined, *What if all the past and present great inventors, poets, and philosophers lived the same life?* No one can get anywhere by analyzing the endless questions of life. That was the path of wastage that I was heading to, and many of us waste our precious time focusing on how to live life rather than just living life. My life was almost consumed by seeking and searching that had no end. It looked to me like the unconscious life is far better than perpetual seeking and searching to become enlightened or reach spiritual fulfillment. I felt I could only get there by accepting that I am already there. I finally decided I am enlightened and conscious enough today and that I am happy and content with my life. All enlightenment and wisdom will come from within now; no time or future accomplishment is necessary.

That decision to stop searching led me to immediately stop reading the book I had in my hand. This was because of my contempt of seeking wisdom and enlightenment outside of myself in order to feel complete. I reached a point where I felt that I had read and searched enough and had no more time to waste in searching for anything. I found God in that moment and in this lifestyle of mine with all the imperfections. I do not wish to see God in any other state of mind or lifestyle at a future date. Let all my wisdom, poems, truths, enlightenment, and consciousness come to me in this very moment and state of mind, or I absolutely do not need them. These qualities are here with me now at this very moment. I despised the idea of looking forward to a better tomorrow through wasting the present, and I felt, in this very moment, I am one with the infinite intelligence within. This is not a favor that I seek from anyone, and it is not something that will be given to me because of my good behavior, or enlightenment, or wisdom, or the amount of books I read, or my discipline and the time I spend on meditation. As a matter of fact, I reduced the time I was spending on meditation to prove this point. I said enough with life-consuming thoughts and teachings that tell you, "You are not good enough." I said to myself and the universe, "Take me as I am!" Nothing will ever make me deserving of grace. I am already in a state of grace, regardless of my lifestyle and situations. It is the ego that creates this illusion of seeking the grace through living a particular way or gaining a certain level or wisdom in order to receive grace. We just have to recognize and accept this truth and have trust in the existence of grace within us. I hope this book will guide you into discovering the abundant power, grace, treasures, and intelligence within you. Your conditions and situations have no power to bestow you with this eternal grace or take it away from you. Your simple recognition will make you see and experience this grace. Once you recognize this truth, you cannot un-recognize it, but your unconscious life can create the illusion of lacking this grace. I believe that knowing this truth will set you free.

Many people who achieve extraordinary success in life are those who have overcome personal challenges. This is what Steve Jobs called the "gap" in one of his televised interviews. This allows you to see beyond the conventional or ordinary world. After deeply looking within, you become one with your spiritual world, and creativity oozes out of you. I am extraordinarily blessed and lucky to have been given the opportunity after what other people would term as challenges or failures, and now I call them blessings. I think the challenges teach you to look at life differently and give you that gap to step back and change your perspective. So, much is expected from me because I was blessed with so many incredible experiences as a result of the challenges and soul-searching I went through. I was given the wisdom to transmute my struggles to opportunities.

My past unconscious life is part of the journey to enlightenment. It is as important as the enlightened or conscious part of my life. This journey started right from the time I was born. All the events led me to the purification of my soul and shading off of what is not life. Each part of the journey is as important as the other. I must have supremely played my past role of unconscious life; that is how I got my ideas and life perspectives I share in this book. At the time, the past life looked like a failure and meaningless, but that was the path that led me to purification. I hope to impart those lessons to other people who are going through challenging times.

One of the main teachings of this book is personal responsibility; it means not blaming other people, God, or the devil for the problems in your life. This responsibility comes with empowerment and wisdom. You will have a better understanding of the power and effects of your thoughts, beliefs, and faith. It will teach you to find enlightenment and right-mindedness in your current circumstances or life situation, and this will enable you to discover and use your power to create a good life for yourself and others. Your life's problems are not because you don't have power or because you don't have faith; they are mainly because you don't have the right-mindedness or knowledge of the universal laws.

Opinion of Others versus Self-Confidence

Self-Confidence

One of the most important character attributes
To have in life is courage and confidence.
No matter what you do or who you are,
Confidence is vital in your endeavor.

If you lose your job because you refused to be intimidated
Or, because of your confidence, your boss is perturbed
And wants you to break down and feel inferior and subdued,
Stand your ground and never compromise your self-worth.
You will find a better job that accepts your courage.

If you lose your marriage because your spouse
Undermines yourself worth and confidence,
Don't be afraid to walk away to start a better life.
If you have people around who are offended by your confidence,
Then offend them more, for they don't deserve to be your friends

If there are people around you who are not confident

And you bring down yourself to look like them,
Then you are destroying yourself and the little confidence they have.
Instead, lift them up to the throne you all deserve.

I prefer to eat grass and live with animals than lose my confidence
To keep my job or the false comfort of life.
I prefer to sleep in caves than lose my confidence
To keep my home or job or the illusory status.
Why are we so afraid? Why do we bring down ourselves,
Giving away our dignity and self-worth for others' sake?

Show me a woman or a man whose life is miserable
Because he or she is too confident and remained respectable,
But I will show you countless people who lead a miserable life
Because they lacked confidence to stand up for themselves.

Be the first man to die of hunger and poverty
Because you refused to sell your integrity.
It has never happened, and it never will.
You have one life to live and live it well.
The worst thing in life is not material poverty
But loss of one's worth and a spiritual bankruptcy.

Material wealth can come and go or change over time.
In bad or good times, your spiritual wealth will thrive.
If you have spiritual wealth, you are always rich,
Happy, confident, and healthy, so heavens you can reach.

It is the best wealth you can have in this world,
And every other blessings and success will come.
There is no single justification for our fear and lack of confidence,
For all of us were gifted with this eternal grace.

It is not given to one person more and to another less,
But the difference is in how much dirt has covered our grace.
How much have you covered the sunshine within your chest?
And prevented yourself from becoming the best?
How much talent are you holding back from the world
By preventing confidence from shining through your heart?

Confidence is not something you gain from without.
It is already there within. Just remove the dirt.
Bring out the eternal light and make your world bright.
A victory is guaranteed, so don't give up the fight.

The Truth about Self-Confidence and Self-Esteem

Self-confidence means what you think of yourself, the opinion you have about yourself. It is never about the opinion of others about you or what they think of you. You are at the center, and nobody else is at the center with you. Self-confidence is purely what you think of yourself. As other people are entitled to their thoughts, you are also entitled to yours. The only thought you should care about at all is yours. That means the world to you, and that is your only and primary world. You live there. Your confidence lives there.

You can control only your thoughts. What others think of you should not be your concern. They also live in the mental world that they chose create. Take care of your world and let them take care of theirs. Your self-confidence comes from within and flows outward, never from without to within. So never expect other people to boost your self-confidence or give it to you.

The mistake we always make is we look at self-confidence as a measure of how and what people think of us. We think in terms of how people see us, whether they see us as confident or not confident. Therefore, we say to ourselves, "They think I am confident," or otherwise. We are only concerned about how people think of us rather than what we think of ourselves. It is not about our confidence that we worry, but it is what people think of our confidence that we worry about. You create your self-image based on how people see you or what they say about you. So, if in the past people described you as lacking self-confidence, then you adopt those opinions to create an identity for yourself.

Your self-confidence is always there; it is part of your nature and everybody's. As kids, we were not aware of other people's judgments, so we played and acted without much concern about their opinion. We never thought about having or not having self-confidence. Your self-confidence never leaves you, even when you thought you lacked it. Instead, the shining power of your self-confidence depended on how much you covered it with the opinion of others. The times that you feel less confident are because you are reflecting on the opinion of others and what you believe they are thinking of you rather than the absence of self-confidence. It is the opinion of others that you are worried about, and that worry just veils your self-confidence more. If you don't see the blue sky or the sun covered by the cloud, your doubt cannot make them disappear. Your ignorance cannot change a fact but just gives you the wrong perception, and likewise, your understanding cannot change the fact that inalienable self-confidence exists within you.

The truth is that you can only control what you think and not what other people think of you or the world. You cannot control how much confidence other people think you have. People's opinions change frequently, and they have thousands of thoughts a day. What they think is their right, and all you should focus on is what you think about yourself and your self-image. Worrying about the opinions of every person that you come across disintegrates your soul. You will not have an anchored faith and foundation from which your self-image is created. This results in frequent change of self-confidence, depending on the opinion of others and whether they say things to you that make you feel better or bad. This inconsistent self-confidence invariably fails and makes your worthiness dependent on others. You seek approval from others to make you feel confident, happy, and worthy. It is like you are begging from others for what you already have inside. All that you have to do is to remind yourself and recognize that your self-confidence is within, and nobody can give it you or take it away from you. When begging for self-confidence, people only give you fake currency; when you take it to the bank or the market, you will be disappointed. The self-confidence you have been seeking from others is not real; that is why it is not consistent or lasting. The begging and seeking only increases the layers of dirt that are veiling your true self-confidence from shining.

Change how you look at self-confidence and change your world. It will never be the same again. You should live your life with full acceptance and joy, without worrying about the opinion of others. You should not worry about what others think about your career, job, speech, poems, voice, name, origin, dressing style, gender and gender affiliation, lifestyle, accent, education, marital status, and of course your self-confidence.

Nothing you accomplish in this world will give you self-confidence, and no one in this world can give you self-confidence, however they are willing to do so. Do not seek any activity, career, wealth, talent, job, people, religion, or even knowledge to give you self-confidence or self-worth. No one can give it to you, and no one can take it from you, but you can deny yourself self-confidence through your ignorance. The denial doesn't mean that it was taken away from you, but instead, you have covered it up by false beliefs and perceptions. The moment you get the awareness that it is already within, then the veils will start peeling off, and self-confidence will start shining.

Focusing on What Others Think of Us

We sometimes care so much about the opinion of others that we base our thoughts and actions on what they think of us. That will lead to complete abandoning of the infinite intelligence within you and your intuitions. You should instead dwell on what you think of yourself; that is the most important thing, and that is the most important opinion in the world. So why should we waste our time worrying, thinking, and caring about what others think of us? Why do we waste our precious time and life dwelling on others' opinion? That is the most wasteful thing to do. The fact that you let other people's opinion and actions hurt you or determine your worth means that you do not value the opinion you have of yourself. The only opinion in the world that can hurt you or bless you is yours. Show that you value your own opinion by not giving unnecessary attention to others' opinion. A lot of people do not have good opinion of themselves, so the opinions they have of you reflect how much they value themselves.

When all your life you struggle to fit into what others expect of you or their opinion, then who are you? You come out of life like a mud sculpture that was made by everybody who walked past it; everybody threw a piece of mud at it, and nobody can even figure out or guess what it will look like in the end.

Stop living as an product of people's opinion. That will withdraw all of life's forces from you. This is a result of worry, pretentiousness, expectations, conformity, and fear, and these emotions are not part of your nature. These are impurities and unnatural emotions that develop as a result of our ignorance and separation from the infinite intelligence within. The emotional challenges and pain you experience are as a result of these unnatural and artificial emotions created by your ego.

You will always have worthy opponents along the way in this life who will challenge you and make you a better and stronger person. Youi will be misunderstood, ridiculed, betrayed, laughed at, called a fool, looked down upon, hated or disrespected, racially discriminated, doubted, or rejected, but none of these opinions, actions, or behaviors matter. Live in your own world and do not dwell on the opinions of others. What people say is an explanation of who they or what they feel rather than who you are.

Dominant Opinions

What you are is determined by your daily dominant thoughts and habits. There are no surprises or luck that will nudge you out of your orbit of thoughts to make you become someone else. Your daily thoughts and the opinions you have of yourself will shape your destiny. What do you imagine and what do you think of yourself? Do you see yourself as a strong or weak person, as smart or a fool, as poor or rich, as happy or unhappy? Whatever imagination and thoughts you dwell on, you become. How you see yourself is the powerful seed that grows into who you are in life. It is not the opinions of your teachers, parents, friends, or mentors that will determine who you are; it is your own opinion.

The difference between your opinion and opinions of others about you is like the difference between the sun and candlelight. Your opinion has the power of the sun, and the opinion of others has the power of the candlelight. Which one shines more? Which one has more power? Do not major the minor and minor the major. Do not overlook the power that you have and sabotage yourself. There is nothing more important or powerful outside you that can shape your world. You are the master of your destiny. Why do you wish to be the slave or servant of others' opinion? Take responsibility and control of your life. Ruling the world means nothing. The most important is being the master of your own kingdom. It is the most powerful, most rewarding, most influential, and most prestigious position and authority you can have in this world. No leadership position or job is better than this.

Opinion of Others and Attack

When you care too much about the opinions of others and you let it disturb your peace of mind, then you will start having thoughts of attack and anger against those whose opinion you care about. This is because at some point you will start perceiving that they have unfavorable or negative opinions of you. Do you see how illusion works? The same people whose opinion you care about are the same people you want to attack. If in the end you don't like them, why should you care about their opinion?

So next time you are tempted to care about others' opinions, remember you may end up hating or attacking them. All these thoughts of attack and lack of peace are going to waste your time and energy. Do not waste the precious moment or your life. Do not waste your energy on these illusions.

We are easily enslaved by other people's faults or weaknesses by dwelling on the other person's weaknesses and shortcomings and hence losing precious moments—or even our entire lives if we are not careful. You would do better by dwelling on their positive sides and divinity rather than their weakness. That would be good for you and the other person. That is the life of wisdom. The positive thoughts you have about others will benefit you more than they will benefit them. It is a win-win for everybody. The benefit of positive thoughts for our bodies and minds are scientific facts.

The Girl with the Addiction Problem

I watched this young girl explaining to a news reporter that she easily gets addicted to everything—to Facebook and then drugs and so on. She believed or was told that she is weak and easily gets addicted to things or substances. At twenty-two years old, she is now on the street of BC-Surrey, addicted to fentanyl and other drugs. It is sad to see how our false beliefs and the opinions of others about who we are can easily lead us to self-destruction and low self-esteem.

She believed in the illusion of lacking self-control, and she succumbed to it. We should be especially careful of what we say to our kids or young people because they can easily create an identity for themselves out of those conversations.

The Ego's "Forgetful" Identity

The ego sometimes tries to give you an identity based on harmless and frivolous errors, such as the times you forgot your car keys or forgot to lock a door. Based on these simple errors, some people give themselves a permanent identity as a forgetful person. The false identification will create your reality of chronic forgetfulness and self-doubt. Even before forgetting anything, when preparing for a trip, gym, or work, you will always ask yourself if you have forgotten something. It is much better to actually forget than have those thoughts about yourself. You know when you abandon these thoughts, you actually realize that you rarely forget things; it was the ego trying to exaggerate those rare moments you actually forgot. Sometimes, people suggest that you are a forgetful person, and you believe their opinions and make it a reality in your life.

What If

What if the imaginary fear and concern about the opinion of others is just a form of mental illness that is benign and assumed as normal because a great majority of human beings suffer from it? That is a real possibility. The greatest tragedy is not death but never starting to live. You have not started living if you still suffer from this illusion. The cure is just the realization of the illusion that the ego created and removing it through conscious observation.

The people who realized and observed this are successful in whatever field they chose to pursue. The majority of the people are just suffering from the condition silently. Many died without fulfilling their dreams and without living their lives fully. The imaginary concerns and fear drowned their true potential.

There is this high table of success that I imagine the people who have supreme confidence in expressing themselves occupy. This table consists of individuals who are not afraid to express themselves and are not afraid of criticism. They take nothing personally and do not let the opinions of others affect their confidence or work. They have learned how to appreciate and accommodate other people with high energies of life like themselves. They do not see other people's confidence as threatening to them or their confidence as being rude to others. They are loud, cheerful, and spontaneous, and they fearlessly express themselves. They are not concerned if what they are saying is correctly perceived by others or if it conflicts with others' beliefs or opinions. They are not self-critical; they are relaxed and confident.

Do not feel threatened by confident people but admire and appreciate their confidence. That is a positive energy in your brother or sister. You should be grateful to them for bringing that high energy to your environment. Be glad that there is a brother or a sister who is truly living and has overcome illusions.

Let Not Anything outside Determine Your Dazzle

Let not the level of skills you have
Determine how much confidence and dazzle you should have.

Let not the level of material wealth you have
Determine how much confidence and dazzle you should have.

Let not the opinion of others
Determine how much dazzle and confidence you should have.
Let not any external thing
Determine how much confidence and dazzle you should have.

Dazzle and confidence are part of your nature
That is not determined by an external factor.
They are always there even when you are filled with doubts.
They are just veiled but have never left.

The degree of shining power is determined by your thoughts,
By the amount of egoistic and psychological dirt.

Through unconscious life you veiled the infinite
By setting boundaries and thoughts of self-limit.

Some will say, "I will dazzle and be more confident
When I become great in my career, business, or talent."
These thoughts are life wasting and perpetuate discontent.
At first, exercise your intrinsic nature and rights,
And everything else will be at your feet

WHAT IS REAL OR NOT REAL

It is how you are expressing yourself now that matters, not your future or past ways of expression. You are yourself now, as you are. If you are living in shame, guilt, fear, poorly express yourself, or any other forms of scarcity, then you are living like a beggar, weeping for a piece of the world. Look at the blessings and abundance of many in this world. So, why are you living in thoughts of scarcity or why do you feel undeserving of those blessings? You are abundantly blessed, look within and live in faith. Thoughts of abundance are thoughts of gratitude and love and health and healing and God and faith. They are thoughts of peace, happiness, confidence and wealth. These positive dwelling thoughts will create your realities. These thoughts are infinitely greater than the visible material wealth or power.

Thoughts of abundance are thoughts of thankfulness/gratitude. Think as already having NOW wealth, success, health, confidence, courage and all other blessings, whatever you prayed for (your dwelling thoughts) consider them received. Do not ask how, the infinite intelligence will reveal it to you. You should not ask, when, because you should consider it received now.

NB: positive dwelling thoughts/faith should not be thoughts of seeking to have those blessings, but they should be thoughts of accepting/receiving those blessings or as already having them. The later will create a powerful vision and typing on your subconscious mind which will move the universal energy to make it happen.

The seeking will just create lack and perpetual reality of seeking or discontent.

The subconscious mind does not know what is real and not real. Therefore, what is not real in your conscious mind, remains not real in your subconscious mind. What is real in your conscious mind remains real in your subconscious mind. So, the acceptance or considering as received your blessings, means you see those blessings as real in your conscious mind. So here, the most important thing is your conscious decision of accepting or choosing what is real or not real in your life. The real and not real are simply the creations of your conscious mind (thinking mind). Hence, your perception of what is real or not real, creates your external reality.

It is very simple idea, but infinitely powerful. You see, when you just read about this truth, as I did in the past, you don't get that deep understanding/revelation. But when it is revealed to you, you deeply understand the wisdom as eternal truth, you just feel or experience it. Reading it or mental understanding is same as reading about sushi, you read or someone tells you that sushi tastes great, but you don't know what kind of taste the sushi has, since you have not tested it. On the other hand, revelation/deep understanding or spiritual understanding or experienced wisdom or knowledge is like actually tasting the sushi that you read about. It is seeing through spiritual eyes, it is the only way of understanding and gaining true knowledge/wisdom that are eternal and instantly and forever stay with you. You don't get them by cramming or repeatedly reading or analyzing them, none of them will give you the true taste of sushi like actually tasting it. What is real or not real in your conscious mind will be eventually created as your external reality by your subconscious mind. So, the real and most important stage of creations takes place in your conscious/thinking mind (invisible creation), the subconscious mind just executes the order but cannot make any choices and does not have the to power to reject the choices you made.

What is real/not real, possible/impossible are all in your power, that is what we call infinite power. What you said and thought as real/possible in your life becomes real/possible in your life. Likewise, what you said and thought as not real/impossible in your life, becomes impossible/not real in your life. These are eternally true, Simple as that. It is not society/culture/traditions/education or people's opinion that set for you what is possible or not possible. They didn't set that for Mohammed Ali, Barrack Obama, Henry Ford, Steve Jobs, Bill Gates, Einstein, Wright Brothers, etc. for the society, everything all these people did was impossible or not real, only themselves decided what is real or not real, what is possible or not possible in their lives. The society only sees their manifestations later and accept them as real or possible.

So, you see, how some make billions of dollars in a day and others live in abject/extreme poverty or in a mountain of debt. How others can create, manage and lead several multi billion-dollar companies and others fail to even perform the simplest tasks that their mediocre job demands. Both groups of individuals decided or chose what they can or cannot do, what is possible or not possible.

It is amazing with all those years of schooling, I didn't know these truths. No wonder the majority of the world's population live in poverty. If a guy with master's degree was so ignorant, unenlightened, unconscious and wrong-minded, what do you expect from others who have little or no education?

"knowledge/information is power" so true, so true, my friends. All immortal souls, first saw themselves as who they are and what they are and what they can do, accepted/recognized their gifts/power/blessings as received before anyone/society can see or recognize those things in them. No man or woman, society or circumstances can create or decide who you are, only you can. It comes from within, then flows without. All our worry, fear, anxiety, doubts, scarcity or lacks are because we wrongly thought other people, society or circumstances create, decide or determine who we are or what kind of life or level of success, love, abundance we can have. Therefore, we end up wasting our life, time and energy trying to shape their opinion or approval so that they can create a successful or abundant 'us'. 'Me' creates 'me', not 'you' create 'me'. This misconception/ illusion of others creating you, has resulted or results in you begging from others, for love, job/career growth, income for life's necessities, positive self-image, level of success or abundance, happiness, peace of mind, confidence, courage, good health etc. We seek from others what they cannot give us and most of the time, those people do not have these things themselves. Stop the begging, the begging eyes, the begging voice, the begging habits or behaviours. You are abundantly powerful and blessed, express this fact, through your way of talking, walking, seeing, writing or singing, let your behaviours habits and thoughts reflect this truth, let your whole life or existence be a testimony of this truth. Let your decision-making process and actions be a testimony of this truth. Let your health, wealth, success, happiness, peace of mind, confidence, courage and contentment be a testimony of this truth.

NB: you can accept/recognize this truth in the present moment or the now only. Accepting/receiving what s real to you now, is more important than the eventual visible reality.

It is not the external hell that burns you most hard, but it is the internal hell that will cause you unimaginable misery or burn (mentally created by you or your perception). It is not the external heaven that will give you the greatest happiness, peace of mind, wealth or contentment but it is the internal heaven (your positive dwelling thoughts and choice of what is real to you).

Why sometimes, it is easy to see others as they are and challenging to see yourself as who you are or who you want to be? Because, you have lived for a very long time in illusion of who you are or your old identity (that is why it is said, you are your own greatest enemy). Also, you only witness what others created as their reality or who they are in their external manifestation, this is the final stage of creation and therefore easy to accept as you can see them with your necked eyes.

Your ego's illusions look too real because of years of confirmation and acceptance by yourself. Admiring and focusing on external manifestation of others (on TV and social media) and just getting carried away by daily demands of life, will lead you in to ignoring conscious creation of what is real to you. Religious beliefs and cultures, your parents' and friends' opinions of who you are, ignorance, giving of power to your circumstance and conditions to shape who you are (changing faces), lack of faith and teachings of society and schools on preconditions of success, they set for you what is possible and impossible, what is real and not real etc. which you ignorantly followed in the past. This created layers of illusions that seem impossible to remove. Break away and fly out. It is a universal and eternal truth, no one or nothing can stop you or limit you or create boundaries of what you can achieve. You are the master of your own destiny and fate. That is how the truth will set you free, free from any bondages or enslavement by others opinions, limits, impossibilities, and boundaries. You are a free spirit, spread your wings of imagination and creativity and fly.

Bring Dazzle and Confidence to Your Work

You bring dazzle and confidence to your work, talent, or any other activities in your life. You don't get confidence and dazzle out of these activities. If you are waiting to be confident and dazzle once you become good in your profession, activities, or talents, you will be waiting in vain and die a miserable person who never really lived a good life. You will die waiting to live.

Dazzle and confidence are part of every human being's nature. Over time, you veiled these qualities unconsciously due to experiences in life and wrong teachings from society. Just remove the veils, and it will come out shining.

Live your life with confidence and dazzle now. Do not wait for anything in life so that you can have these qualities, which are part of your nature. The only way to reach your goals in life is by realizing that you can get there through self-confidence and dazzle. If you don't have it now, nothing else will give it to you in the world.

No amount of wealth or skills will provide you with self-confidence. You seek self-confidence outside yourself for years and years, but you will never find it because you already have it inside. Instead, simply remove the veils that prevented it from shining and manifesting in your life.

Can you ask a table to hand you a paper that is on it? You can stand there and yell at the table for hours or days, but it will never hand you the paper. The same way, you cannot expect to get self-confidence from activities that you perform or talent, profession, or education. You can scream and beg for the activities or occupations to give you confidence, but you will end up unfulfilled and discontented.

You pick the paper from the table. Your talent or profession is the table, and your confidence and joy are the act of picking up or putting a paper on the table. You bring confidence and dazzle to your activities but do not expect the activities or anything external to hand you confidence and dazzle.

The ego will tell you, you have to wait for that moment or special task, place, or wealth or position or state of mind to be courageous. But the truth is that you can exercise courage everywhere and in everything you do in your current position. You should courageously breathe, look, eat, drink, work, dream, laugh, love, and talk. You should do these things courageously and from time to time observe yourself doing it.

The unconscious life is the absence of courage through veiling or covering with illusion of lack. All the good characters or qualities I talk about are the manifestation of the qualities of God within you. These qualities are not privileges to some but an intrinsic right to all.

In everything you do, add the miraculous spice of courage. Are you walking? Walk courageously. Are you writing? Then write courageously. Are you speaking? Then speak courageously. Are you working? Then work courageously. That is the meaning of true living; otherwise the years in your life are empty. Money, fame, and fortune are nothing if you don't live courageously, and you need none of them to live courageously. You do not have to wait to live courageously; it is now or never. The biggest lie is waiting for things to get better in order to live a life of courage. But it is courage that will make things better, or you will die without really living. Did you see the gymnast jumping and doing acrobatics on the beam at the Olympics? And yet you walk as if you will fall off this earth. Walk with pride, walk with confidence, and walk with courage.

Courage attracts favors like success, love, happiness, peace, prosperity, blessings, wisdom, wealth, abundance, and strength. These are some of the qualities that courage attracts to you. Fear attracts the opposite of all these. True living means courage; fear and cowardice are illusions that are wasting the lives of many.

I watched on *48 hours*, a TV program, about a woman whose husband was killed. In attempt to cover up her little financial deceit and greed, she let her husband's killer, who is a lawyer, get away with the murder. The perpetrator was also awarded a $5 million fine for false accusation. The killer didn't only get away with the murder but also got a financial reward for her crime. In life, you will find a lot of people who are abused and mistreated because of their cowardice and greed. You have to master the courage of standing up for yourself and justice.

Peace of Mind—Abandoning the Opinion of Others

It is ridiculous to imagine that people care so much about your thoughts. People are not even aware of the changes taking place in your mind, and they don't care. Yet you are worried and concerned about what people think of you or the spiritual changes you are going through. Do not live your life worrying about others' opinions. It is like a fish frantically jittering on the sand after getting thrown out of the water. And the fish has this illusion of all the other fish coming to the shore to watch his struggle. Of course, not even a single fish is near the shore; they are all in the water swimming and minding their own business. Everyone is minding their own business, so focus on yours. Your thoughts matter only to you and nobody else in this world. Your thoughts are your world, and the same way, other people's thoughts create their worlds, so you should quit trying to reconcile the two worlds. That can never happen.

You cannot reside in the thoughts of others; they can only have a passing glimpse of you that lasts for seconds or minutes. Similarly, you cannot dwell on the opinion of others or their thoughts. You live in your world; trying to escape it or attempting to substitute it by preoccupying your mind with other people's opinions will just drive you to more illusions.

The only time this insanity stops is realizing that the only world you control is yours. The only thought you control is yours. Stop worrying about what other people think of you or their opinion; that is when the fragmentation stops, and you become whole. You become one with the spirit in you. Your spirit, character, and thoughts then become solid through the union. Nothing in the world can stand before you. You just have to observe the thoughts and worry you are experiencing as wasteful illusions that should be ignored without attention or self-judgment, and soon enough, the illusion will disappear. That cannot happen in the future or the next moment but only now. Remind yourself to focus on the present moment.

Better Courage Takes Me to Hell Than Fear Takes Me to Heaven

Stop oscillating and being too cautious when making decisions. The egoistic mind has been exaggerating the importance of everyday little things as if they were life-and-death matters. You have in the past wasted a lot of time doubting your decisions and over evaluating your choices regarding the simplest things in life. A lot of people are stuck because they fear making mistakes. What mistakes? It is not like you are making life-and-death decisions every day. Live your life as if nothing is a mistake and it is impossible for you to make a mistake. Even the mistakes you make come with a lesson, and it shows you that you have made an effort to take a step or do something, but self-doubt and oscillation have no benefits at all. That is the real mistake and the only mistake you can commit. Wasting time or doubting yourself or oscillating is life wasting and the worst mistake you can make. Why all these doubts for this short life?

Self-doubt is life corroding, such that you will not accomplish much in life because you keep checking again and again if you are doing the right thing. This is an illusion of the ego, which made you believe that you are not good enough to accomplish this or that. The ego makes you think that an average person like you is not good enough to accomplish any great things.

Watching Kipchoge Keino at the Rio Olympics

In the Rio Olympics opening, Kipchoge Keino was given the first and one of the most prestigious awards in the Olympics for his work supporting orphaned children. He was being watched by billions of people all over the world. His English or speech was not good at all, but it didn't matter to me because his presence on that stage was enough.

This was a man who was not supposed to be on any stage to speak. He was not supposed to be there, just like I am not supposed to write a book. That was the biggest inspiration for me. A lot of us waste our years trying to give people the best impression of who we are, trying to shape their opinion of who we are. This is an endeavor that has no end and a game that you will never win.

Confidence and Faith to Achieve Success

Confidence and courage also mean you are confident and sure of the presence of the infinite intelligence, power, abundance, wealth, happiness, health, peace, faith, and convictions within you. It means you have great conviction in the laws of the universe, God, and the abundant presence of love, courage, contentment, enlightenment, wisdom, talents, and all other good things in your life. You are sure of the green pastures, you are sure of your *dhabbinn*, you are sure of the laws that govern the universe, and you are sure of yourself.

This is how the greatest sages, poets, philosophers, artists, scientists, inventors, and most powerful and rich people have felt and feel. This is the greatest confidence you can have. All of them had one thing in common across all ages and generations: they had the greatest faith, confidence, or conviction. They had nothing else in common; they all lived in different times or centuries or civilizations, they had different upbringings, they had different skills, they had different pasts, they had different lifestyles, they had different levels of education, they had different religions, all of them were born in different countries and eras, they all looked different, they didn't have a conventional education or path to follow, and they created their own paths. The only tool they had to achieve great things in their lives was their faith. They did not first seek external qualifications, skills, education, or money to achieve great things or change the world; they sought and depended only on their faith, conviction, or confidence. They sought the kingdom of God first, and the rest came. Only if you want to achieve and live a mediocre life would you first seek external conditions and fulfillments. Every greatness is born of great faith and conviction. That faith soon manifests itself as external reality that people see and marvel at.

2

Self-Expression and Public Speaking

Self-Denial

The ability to express and speak the truth in our everyday lives
Is as important as fighting for our other constitutional rights
That we value and demand from governments and institutions,
But this time, we demand those rights from ourselves.

Among the basics of human rights is to speak our minds.
No matter who we face and no matter who disagrees,
We should stand for our convictions and beliefs
That anchor our behaviors and deeds.

If you completely denied yourself this basic right
For so many years in the past,
Because of pure cowardice or to just look a part,
And you always lived with eagerness to please others,

This should be a measure of your success in life,
To express yourself without fear of a loss,
A loss of friendship or a loss of social status,

However your truth displeases others.

You live in this free country, and yet you were never free.
No one but you denied yourself these rights
To largely maintain fake social harmony and outdated beliefs
That enslaved the minds of many for centuries.

How can you ever claim to be a free man
When you didn't have the courage to speak your mind?
How you ever worried that a government or an institution
Would take away or suppress your freedom of expression
When you absolutely ignored your ideas and intuitions?

How for all these years you lived with wanton self-negligence.
How your eyes were closed to this injustice to self by self.
You cannot change the past, and don't regret what happened.
But at this moment, at this time and going forward,
Promise yourself to exercise your rights
Of expressing your ideas without fear and judgment.

Self-Expression versus Public Speaking

Many people make the mistake of focusing on and practicing public speaking when they should focus on getting better in day-to-day conversation. Improve your day-to-day conversations and you will inadvertently become a great public speaker. What are the chances of you making public speeches daily or regularly, and what are the chances of you talking to people on a daily basis? Of course, you have conversations every day, so take each opportunity to perfect your communication skills.

To become a great public speaker, you should first become great in your everyday conversation. Your private conversations are the primary foundation of your public speaking skills. How do you dream of speaking well in front of strangers when you cannot speak well in front of your colleagues and family members and friends? That is where public speaking begins. In your everyday conversation, you have countless chances to perfect your public speaking skills.

Trying to master public speaking confidence without working on your daily conversations is building your house on sand. It is like learning how to fake confidence for only those moments in front of people. Do not target the symptoms but the root causes of the disease, as that is true healing.

The Illusion of the Introvert

As in many other cases of false identity created by the ego, this also is a result of a negative self-image. It is the illusion of the ego to see itself as an introvert that strengthened the lie. It is a label and false identity the ego created to explain past experiences and opinions. It is the ego that was trying to create an identity for itself by referencing your past experiences and behaviors that were just temporary, and now the ego wants to make a permanent identity out of those experiences. The fact that you feared something in the past does not make you fearful of that same thing for the rest of your life. We all had some fears as kids, but do we create our identity based on those fears we had as kids? As grown-ups, we now see those fears as childish. But how is it then possible for us to form our identity based on some past experience or our reactions to certain events? That is the egoistic mind trying to give a permanent identity based on referencing and selective memory. The fact that you responded in a certain way in the past to a certain external stimulus does not mean you give yourself an identity out of that experience or you allow other people to give you an identity based on those responses. The introvert identity that you were trying to protect or overcome or change is not even you but a label you gave yourself or others gave you based on one time or a few experiences in the past.

How can you struggle to change what is not you or what is not in you in reality? Do you think of yourself as a baby who needs breastfeeding or a bottle of milk because you once used to do that? Do you think of yourself as that baby now? So, if you decide to label yourself and identify yourself based on your past experiences and actions, then which one are you of the millions past experiences? Why are you fixated on a few identities that you picked based on your past responses or opinions of others? Grow up spiritually and recognize the fallacy of these identities.

The way you interpreted your past experiences and opinions of others formed your current identity and reality. People sometimes gave you those identities or opinions to make you conform, make themselves more important and intelligent, to get something from you, or for other egoistic and self-centered purpose. Now I am telling you Santa is not real, and neither are those negative self-images and identities. Don't give recognition to those false identities by trying to fight them or by analyzing them. They never existed in reality, so how do you change them? Just let them go as you would let go the existence of Santa.

Because of your past false identity as an introvert, do not let that experience determine how you speak now or in the future. That was not you; observe and ignore these illusions every time the past feelings and thoughts of poor self-expression come to your mind.

Celebrity Blessing

The most important blessing of the celebrities is not their wealth or fame but their ability to express themselves supremely. And that is a blessing all of us have. It is given to all of us equally. The difference is to what degree you allow the infinite intelligence to shine in the form of self-expression. Just remove the veil that is stopping the infinite intelligence from shining. Once you allow this blessing to shine, all the other blessings will follow.

The quality of your life depends on the level of your confidence in self-expression. If you live without supremely expressing yourself, then you died without living a supreme life. You need no education or any special knowledge or voice to express yourself. The people who are good at expressing themselves are not any more special than you. They possess no special skills, but they practiced and had the courage to express themselves. You will surprise yourself with how good you are at expressing yourself if you master the courage of doing so without worrying about the opinions of other people.

Self-expression, whether in the form of public speaking or private conversation, is a very important ingredient for success. It does not matter what you are talking about, if you are knowledgeable in that field or not, if you have a good voice or not, if you speak that language fluently or not, or if your accent is good or not. You will deliver a great speech or conversation if you courageously and fearlessly express yourself. You will manifest the qualities of the infinite intelligence within you, which will give you guidance to make your points or thoughts clearly.

Just like speaking, writing is a supreme kind of self-expression. Public speaking is only one kind of self-expression; others are music, sports, and other forms of art and creative work. You will see the expression and a glimpse of the person's identity through their work.

Books saved my life when I was younger and thought of committing suicide. Those dark days, I came across some books that literally stopped me from committing suicide. I hope my book will help others love themselves and see the good in everything. I just want to remind people of the treasures they have within. I hope to inspire many through my book just the same way I was inspired. I do not need to be excellent in the English language or have an English degree to explain my intuitions and ideas clearly.

Brothers

There is a form of brotherhood (including women) among those who have realized their true identity rather than bonds based on race or religion. They are people who are in harmony with their spirit, those with supreme confidence and courage. The ones who know their true identity or the infinite intelligence within. They transcend color, race, religion, background, and skills. They have realized the wonders and blessings of believing in themselves. Those are brothers in the realm of the spiritual world. The interviews on news TV, *Ellen*, and *Oprah* are the celebrations of you joining the brotherhood. It's the symbol of your victory over self-limiting illusions.

Do you expect Bill Maher to work at McDonald's or any other small job? No matter the level of education, English skills, background, experience, network, or godfathers he has, this guy would have risen to the highest level in any field. Those qualifications and criteria I mentioned are the ones that an average person uses for getting or not getting a job. But in reality, they are not that important.

There is no way, you could speak with that much confidence and yet work in a low-level job. You will soon rise to the top of any field you pursue, and nothing in the world can stop you.

The same goes for other TV hosts, speakers, comedians, movie stars, CEOs, televangelists, spiritual teachers, and political leaders. Your courage and confidence will decide how far you go. It is your own courage rather than anything outside that will determine your success.

3

The Two Energies

The Two Sources of Energy

There are people in your life who bring you positive energy
And make you feel good and make this life lively,
And there are people who make you feel bad about yourself and life,
Bring the negative energy, abuse you, treat you badly,
Deny you the opportunity in life, or make you sad.

It's the people who challenge you, who will make you a great person,
These are the people who give you valuable lessons.
But remember you don't want to be in their class for long,
For life is not about learning lessons all the time.
Learn from the experience and move on with your life.

And be grateful for the lessons from each source.
Just like a magnet has both the north and south pole,
Life has both the positive and negative energy.
You cannot have a magnet without both poles,
And you cannot have life without the two sources.

Our world is beautiful and perfect as it is,
And it cannot exist in any other way, I believe.

Both positive and negative energies in life
Are as important as the other and have their purpose.

Nothing was made to hurt you but to make you stronger.
Do not take anything personally. They all exist as they are.
Learn to love and accept them for what and who they are.

Life does not always give you what you want
But always gives you what you need,
To make you a better person indeed.
The world cannot be more perfect,
And you cannot be more perfect.
Treat each day as your best.
Welcome each source of energy as a guest
That came to bless and make your life great.
Love them all because you love yourself.

Why Do You Allow Your Day to Be Poisoned?

Many of us live our lives depending on the moods, thoughts, and reactions of others. That is the worst form of slavery. Most people cannot even control what they think about themselves and hence run into a lot of trouble because they mistakenly believe that they are their mind.

How can you base your life and happiness on their illusions? How can you live your life based on the opinions of others? You become happy when they say or do good things for you and become unhappy when they say or do bad things to you. That is becoming enslaved by the opinions and actions of others.

How can you live a life where you are switched off and on like a light? Switched on and off by every person who comes across or interacts with you. You are sad when they switch you off and happy when they switch you on.

So, your day that would have otherwise been happy, peaceful, productive, and full of energy and creativity is instantly ruined and poisoned by actions or opinions of other people? How foolish and wasteful is that? How can you let another person or event decide whether you are going to have a good or a bad day? You should wake up in the morning and prepare yourself for everything, the good and the bad from others, and remind yourself not to let others take control of your day or mind. Why do you wish to become the slave of every frivolous event and suggestion that takes place during the day? That day could be your last day on earth. Do you want to spend it as a slave? Do you wake up in the morning and ask your colleagues, spouse, friends, or strangers what kind of day you should have? Whether you should have a good or a bad day?

Isn't it wonderful? To always wake up in the morning knowing that you will have peace of mind, love, happiness, and creativity no matter what happens during that day? Nothing and nobody gave you those things, and nobody can take them away from you. Those are truly yours, and they are the most precious things in this world, and you already have them within, and you should not seek them from others.

You are the electric current or the joy that is always there. The switch reflects their mood or need at that moment but does not decide the existence of the electric current. Let them be the bulb that goes off and on depending on their own moods but be the constant current. The electric current is always there whether you see it or not. Your happiness should be like that, always there and always the same.

In every circumstance, look for what opportunities you have to put your principles and philosophies into practice. Every situation will present you with such opportunities. Don't waste these opportunities by focusing on the negative side of the event or the other person.

Look within and ask yourself, what are the opportunities here for me to put my principles and philosophies into action? What happens doesn't matter at all; it is how you respond and make use of the situation that is important.

What happens, happens to everyone all over the world and to many generations throughout human history; hence it is part of nature and never unique to you. What sets us apart and makes us unique is how we respond to what happens. That response can make what happened a blessing or a curse, a fortune or a misfortune, a heaven or hell, a success or a failure. All those choices depend on you, not anybody or anything else. Therefore, these choices make you the master of your life and destiny. Choose the good, virtue, happiness, peace, courage, abundance, blessing, joy, intelligence, calmness, love, gratitude, prosperity, and heaven. Choose wisely; choose wisdom.

All small things that you overlooked to have peace are not for nothing. Nobody is that important to enslave your mind through anger. They can take away anything but not your peace and freedom. Once somebody or something angers you, then you are no longer a free person. Every situation reminds us and calls for a virtue that we identify and use. They are all there for our benefit. Everything happened because we are alive to witness it. All happened because we are blessed with a long life. All happened because we lived another day. Everything happens to make us great or happy. We are stronger because it all happened. Use the challenging people and situations in your life as an alarm that wakes you up to the good and virtue in you. Use them as an alarm that wakes you up to the grace of God within you.

Who are we to want to see only the good in this world? Aren't all the imperfections that make the universe more beautiful? You want to see only a uniformly flat world? It is the valleys, the hills, the mountains, the rivers, the sea, the oceans, the forests, and the deserts that give beauty to our world. Similarly, it is the presence of all kinds of people that make our world more beautiful. Don't the people who differ with you have an equal right to live and behave however they choose? You should be mentally prepared for all kinds of people and behaviors. You are here to live with all, tolerate all, love all, and forgive all.

The openness and mental preparedness to accept people with a negative attitude or low energy will free you from worry and anxiety about dealing with people. Don't be too cautious to meet and befriend people for fear of getting offended by their comments or actions. You cannot refuse to go to the market because some vendors sell rotten or bad oranges. You can't shun society because some people will treat you badly or offend you with their actions.

The true mastery is in your ability to feed off bad energy of others to transmute it to your advantage and not allowing others to decide your reaction by making you angry or perturbed. It is wise to avoid people who bring low energy to your environment, but you cannot run away from all, unless you plan to live a very solitary life in the jungle with animals. Don't let the low energy get to you and think about it afterward; don't let it bother you; don't let the poison into your system. This will make you win the battle before it even began, as you have won the battle over yourself by deciding to have peace within no matter what.

Peace and war come from within. Choose peace. Nobody can choose it for you. No other person's action can dictate how you should feel or respond to a situation; you should be always in charge. Others can be at war with you, but choose peace inside, and that is the most important world. Remain peaceful inside despite the chaos around you, and you will be in a state of peace eternally. Use the wars and chaos to enlighten you. Transmute that energy to make yourself stronger and wiser. How can you win a war against someone who does not have an enemy? If you are at peace with yourself, you will have no enemy.

The one who is at peace with themselves is always serene, calm, and peaceful inside. They don't waste their energy or time by swallowing the poison of anger or other low energies. They transmute all experiences for their own good.

Everything that comes your way should be transmuted to a resource that serves you best. Making use of the other half of the resource that people call "negative" or "bad" as a resource to enrich your life is genius. The use of this other half will enable you to live a full life. Ignoring the other half that people consider bad is a waste of a significant part of your life and a waste of the short time you have on this earth. Life is short; stop wasting half of it.

Accepting Others' Unique Contribution

Just the way we should accept ourselves as we are,
To make our own unique contribution like a star,
We should accept others' uniqueness as well.
This is the other side of the coin in this beautiful life
That we should understand and accept as we strive.

Without the people that we consider "bad" in our lives,
We will not be able to grow or learn more about ourselves.
Without Judas, there would be no salvation for Christians.
We all have Judas in our lives, in the form of people and experiences.

Use hurt and pain as your important teacher
To make you stronger and a better person and a truth seeker.
Every experience in life comes for our own growth and enrichment.
Use the "bad" experiences to bring you closer to enlightenment.

The negative energies are all ingredients
To fulfill an eternal purpose of the universe.
They are not mistakes or sent here by chance,
But they are here to make our world more diverse.

You could never appreciate the good if the bad did not exist.
All these have an eternal purpose: the murderers,
Wars, insults, failures, divorces, deaths, ignorance,
Regrets, abusers, bad jobs, bad bosses, bad marriages,
Thieves, addicts, drugs, bad health, anger, ego, regrets,
Poverty, illiteracy, ignorance, corruption, fear, pain, loss,

Guilt, jealousy, hate, revenge, discomfort, sadness, chaos,
Mass murders, and all the other things you consider evil
Are here for a greater good for all of us. See them as valuable.

Your love should be like the sun, giving light to all.
We should love and accept everyone for who they are.
The earth does not discriminate who should walk on her.
The love you give to others is love you give to yourself;
You receive whatever you gave in return.

I am not talking about the repercussions of doing bad.
I leave that to the laws of the land.
The lesson here is that all that comes your way
Is sent from the heavens for your own good in some way.

It is the universal law and the law that we behold
Dear to our heart that we should accept others' worlds
As we aspire to do the same in our own unique style.
We cannot all be the same; appreciate our differences.

For the heavens, all contribution is equally important,
Though the journeys and the goals are different.
There is no single soul that has no purpose in this world.
It is all perfect as it is, with all the "good" and the "bad."

All the past and the present are just as perfect
As the earth is placed perfectly in its orbit.
The universe had a purpose for you before your birth,
So, do not waste your life judging the contributions of others.

Blame Game and the Illusion of Suffering

Do not waste your life blaming others for your problems, such as
lack of peace or a good job or any other things. You are responsible

for all of them and your life's condition. You created those problems unconsciously, and you can overcome them by being conscious. How can you ever complain and despair of lacking a good job when during those tough times for black people, Frederick Douglass, who was a former slave, rose to become an ambassador and a commissioner? How would you have spent those years if you were an African American who lived during or immediately after slavery?

You fail only if you are fearful, have no peace of mind, or see yourself as a victim of people or institutions. You will fail if you continue blaming other people, depend on others heavily, have low self-esteem, care a lot about other people's opinions, and have no confidence. How will you have any chance to succeed if you cannot overcome these illusions and weaknesses that are holding you back? How can you get anywhere in this state of mind? We do not live in a perfect society, but you are not giving yourself any chance if you cannot fully use your potential by changing your attitude, self-image, or perspectives.

Isn't it bewildering that many people in their heart and world feel and say to themselves, "I have suffered and endured the most in the past"? We have this personal and intimate relationship with the illusion of suffering. How many billions of people have been fooled by this life-eroding illusion? How many come to lay claim to this title of "I suffered the most"? How this ego has consumed countless lives. All the sufferings you are thinking about are just in your mind. It is how you are looking at the world that created this illusion.

I was reading Fox sports news on Twitter about the life of a young British soccer player who was playing for the Liverpool reserve team and ended up in a Paralympic team for his country. He was in a car crash in 2007 that killed two of his friends and put a third one in a coma to date. He was only seventeen at the time of the crash and was left with a permanent disability. I asked myself, How can I complain of what should be and what the future should look like? This amazing young man had a bright future as a professional soccer player and surely had so many other beautiful dreams that were taken away by the horrible car accident in a matter of seconds. He did not let this event break him down and waste his life in sadness feeling sorry for himself; instead, he was determined to make the best out of the situation. He joined the Paralympic team and inspired many others through his determination and great spirit. It also shows how unplanned events or situations cannot break a great spirit. He didn't waste his life as a powerless victim of the car accident; the car crushed his body but not his spirit. He is a true hero and a great role model.

It does not matter where you live or in what condition you live. It is your thoughts that make the place, time, or condition good or bad. Make a habit of having good thoughts about where you live, the time and conditions of your life. All good things will come your way, and you will live a happy life.

Have you seen people who complain that the good times are gone? Then how do they expect good things to happen now? Because even if it happens, they will not have the eyes to see it. I have seen people complain, "When I was in city or country A, everyone said country or city B was the best. So, I always wanted to move to B and finally made a move to B. Now that I am in B, I hear and see all the best things are happening in A. How did I get it so wrong?" It is not the place or the timing that you got wrong, but it is the wrong attitude or perception that you have, and wherever you go, it will surely follow you. Change your perception and you will get the perfect time, place, and conditions. Make your home, career, city, marriage, and time good by having a habit of thinking well of them.

Live as if only good things will come your way, and that is what you will get. Even when what other people call "bad" happens, because of your positive attitude, you will find something that is beneficial to you in any situation. It is our perception that matters; what happens is not that significant.

Self-Acceptance and Love

When you are ashamed of who you are, or afraid that who you are will offend someone you are talking to, then you know you are living the life of a coward. You are ashamed of God and the infinite intelligence within you. You are ashamed of your life and the universe. Say who you are loudly and confidently. Love your life and accept yourself. The negative energy of shame will eat away your entire life through thoughts of feeling inferior to others, based on culture, marital status, wealth, gender, race, religion, beliefs, color, lifestyle, language, or career success. The shame makes you uncomfortable around people and makes you not go out and meet new people because you are ashamed of who you are. You do not want to tell them because you think you are an embarrassment or a failure in life, or you think the other person is better than you. Sometimes this feeling of shame will make you postpone your life until that illusory day in the future when things will get better for you and you feel comfortable telling people about yourself. You keep telling yourself, "Let me fix this," or, "Let me fix that, and then I will be ready to go out and meet people." The only problem about this line of thought is that the perfect day will never come. The ego will keep creating an illusion of more things to accomplish and a sense of unfulfillment until one day you realize your life is gone before you started living it. If you are ashamed of who you are now, you will never be proud of who you will be tomorrow. Do not be ashamed of your weight, gender, accent, color, race, religion, beliefs, lifestyle, marital status, career, wealth status, nationality, health, or level of education. Do not just accept them; be proud of your life and proudly declare who you are without any shame, fear, or hesitation. There is nothing wrong with having a bigger dream or thinking of a better tomorrow, but you will get none of that if you are ashamed of today. Do not waste your days and years in shame. Today, make a promise to yourself to do exactly what you have ignored or postponed because of shame.

It is only the sick eyes that only want to see a perfectly green pasture or landscape, and it is only the sick mind that only wants to see the good things in life and refuses to accept the reality and beauty of this life with all its imperfections. We live in a world where we see health and sickness, wealth and poverty, peace and war, killing and healing, anger and calmness, love and hate, ignorance and wisdom, fairness and unfairness, justice and injustice, stealing and giving. They are all here and make up this beauty we call life. We should not feel remorse or blame ourselves for the unfavorable things that exist but should gladly accept all. We should completely love our lives and existence and circumstances. That is loving your daily life. Love and live each day supremely. Do not focus on your perceived shortcomings but love and be grateful for the blessings you have. You really do not have that much time in this world to talk, think, or complain about how things should be. When you focus on your blessings, grace and joy will follow you always. When you focus on your shortcomings or disadvantages, then you will get more of those things.

How much trouble will we avoid if we reduce or eliminate the idea of wishing that we were someone else, born in a different place and era—that we had different talents, a different skin or culture, a different accent, different kids, different parents, different siblings. Accept the place, time, and circumstances in which nature has placed you as absolutely perfect; these are not your own doing and fighting it will just waste your life and make you a victim of your circumstance. Accept the past, for it is already gone.

The cat doesn't wish she was a tiger and waste her life regretting and wishing she was different. She is just happy where she is. We should accept and love ourselves completely. Working hard to achieve something is different from not accepting yourself or appreciating who you are. You are just as great as the greatest in this world. Just like any other person in this world, you have the infinite intelligence within you waiting to be channeled to achieve your dreams.

No one person is perfect in the eyes of the other, but you should see yourself as perfect in your own eyes.

And the Topic Is Love Today

When you love your life abundantly, you are able to give that love to others or give that love to the rest of the world. You give what you have.

Loving yourself means you love and accept your whole life, including your imperfections, past mistakes, current life and situations, failures, associations, and circumstances. When you love yourself, you love and appreciate whatever skills, talents, wealth, and contribution you have and enhance or leverage them to change your life and the world. That will make you stop the thoughts of ingratitude and the coveting of others' lives while you despise and ignore your life, gifts, and treasures and the power within you that blesses you with infinite abundance.

Why withhold that love from yourself now? You have been telling yourself, or others having been telling you, how you should be ashamed of yourself, that you are a bad person, father, husband, brother, sister, coworker, friend, or student. They have said or thought you are a failure, a sinner, undisciplined, uncaring, and other things that made you hate and despise your life or yourself or feel remorse or guilty about your existence. You may have felt you don't deserve love, grace, happiness, peace, or success. Hold your ground, stay stubborn, and don't let people or circumstances make you hate yourself or feel like less of a human or undeserving. Give yourself all the love in the world first. Nobody else can give it to you, and you cannot give it to anybody if you don't have it yourself. Stay away and don't listen to people who tell you or suggest that you are a bad person and that there is something wrong with you. They think you don't deserve to be alive. When you start loving yourself dearly, you will start noticing and recognizing the good, blessings, abundance, and love in yourself and others. You will accept others as you accept yourself. You will appreciate and enjoy your present moment and stop worrying about the future and stop regrets and guilt about the past. Other feelings of failure, discontentment, and unfulfillment will disappear; happiness will follow you everywhere for the rest of your life.

God is love, so you are love. Not loving yourself is against the universal law. You don't have to accomplish anything to deserve or start loving yourself. Every day, remind yourself how dearly you love yourself despite what is going on in your life. Loving yourself is being grateful. Love will guide you to prosperity, peace, and happiness. When you love yourself, you will start creating good things in your invisible world that will eventually manifest in your visible world, because you will have dwelled on thoughts of abundance, contentment, purpose, success, peace, and happiness. You don't have to see these good things in your visible world in order to start loving yourself. This is a vain and life-wasting attempt of trying to make the universal laws work in reverse. All the creations of love are absolutely good all the time. What good things will come to you or others because you hated or didn't love yourself?

When you don't love yourself, it means you are dwelling on lack, scarcity, discontent, fear, worry, anxiety, and other negative thoughts or self-images. Thus, you are creating these things in your invisible world, and you will soon witness their manifestations in your visible world.

With love, all negative thoughts, emotions, and creations will disappear. Don't seek the positive/good thoughts or emotions in the future or in your future goals. Don't seek your self-worth or whether you deserve love, in the external accomplishments or in the future; you can never find them in external things or at any time in the future. There are all here within you now. All you've ever wanted lies within you, so stop seeking, searching, feeling discontent, and worrying.

Don't think that the negative thoughts or emotions will go away in time; they just get worse while wasting away your present moment. Why would you want to see love, self-worth, success, happiness, contentment, fulfillment, peace, good health, a good self-image, confidence, courage, and abundance other than this day? Today and the present moment is the best day of your life.

You see, you are trying to accomplish great things in life or reach your goals just to feel or experience the same feelings you are denying yourself now. You postponed them to feel them in the future because you ignorantly made them dependent on external accomplishments or a time in the future. It is like you have a bottle of water in your hands while walking in a desert. You postpone drinking the water until you find an oasis somewhere ahead of you. Even after your guide tells you that he will give you another bottle of water each time you finish one and that he can never run out of bottled water to give you, you insist, "I will quench my thirst only after reaching an oasis." In the meantime, you are suffering from thirst and dehydration along the way. You think you only deserve to quench your thirst when you accomplish your goal or reach an oasis. You may even die before reaching the oasis and therefore before drinking the water in your hands. Why suffer in vain? Don't postpone love, success, happiness, abundance, courage, and confidence. They are already in your hands, just like the bottled water. The oasis you see may be a mirage, and your water will not come from it (from external things). Why would you make your journey a suffering? It does no good for you or any other person in this world. Why let the worry of not becoming happy steal your happiness now? Why do you tell yourself, "I will only love myself if I accomplish this or that in the future"? Why are you withholding love and self-worth from yourself now? Why do you set preconditions to love yourself when love never asked for them? Nothing you ever did or will ever do will make you deserving or undeserving of love or self-worth.

Your Very Existence Has Influence

Your very existence has influence on others around you and beyond. So, your life has meaning whether you do something great or not. You cannot choose whether your life will matter or not, but you can choose what kind of influence you want to have. You mattered from the moment you were conceived. You do not have to do anything or become anyone to matter. You do not become more of a human or less of a human because of what you do or what you have; you are a complete human regardless. This is for folks who say, "My life doesn't matter." It matters more than you can ever imagine. The life of a murderer matters as much as the life of a healer, although in a different way.

What Happened the Days You Felt His Absence?

What about those days when you felt God was not with you and the infinite intelligence was not working in you? The days you felt less inspired and filled with egoistic thoughts? What are these days? These days will come and will come many times. But remember this: God has never left you in those moments and can never leave you. Those times you felt his absence are the days you focused on the dirt that veiled you from God. Just remind yourself of the everlasting presence of God in your life. Those are the best moments to remind yourself of his presence and the grace within.

It Is Okay to Have Bad Thoughts

It is okay to have bad thoughts; what is not okay is for you to think that you are bad just because you had bad thoughts. When the bad thoughts occur, just observe them as a wandering of the mind. Observe and ignore them as worthless thoughts that do not require your attention. Do not try to analyze the thoughts and do not fight the thoughts; just observe and then ignore. As the thoughts came to your mind in seconds, they will go away in seconds. Remember the presence of the clouds does not mean the sky is not blue; the clouds will clear away soon, and you will see the blue sky. The dark clouds are not permanent and cannot change the color of the sky or its nature; the dark or bad thoughts are not permanent and cannot change your good nature into bad. Do not create a self-identity out of those short moments of the mind's wandering. Do not dwell on them or analyze these thoughts. Analyzing the thoughts will just produce mental chatter and the development of a new ego. Do not keep score of the good and bad thoughts; this will just waste your time. Instead, accept all that comes to your mind as a temporary wandering away of the mind.

Like Noah's ark, my mind takes in all: the good and the bad, happiness and sadness, fear and courage, peace and war. All are my resources. If I had to write only about the bad or bad times, my book would be half-complete. My book is complete because I write about the good times and the bad times. Both are equally important to me. Both are sources of my inspiration.

Do not feel regret or get angry by looking at your past. Instead, be grateful for the lessons you learned from the past. Marble's beautiful lines and patterns are formed by impurities like silt and iron ore oxides. Your beauty is formed from challenges and emotional impurities and imperfections of the past. See them as things that made you stronger and more beautiful and be grateful. Never choose bitterness, guilt, regret, fear, pain, complain, sadness, self-pity, or hate. Instead, choose love, forgiveness, happy memories, and lessons.

Make your mild yoke to serve you best and become a better person. Joseph, the son of Jacob in the Bible (in the book of Genesis 50:15), did not waste his life on blame, anger, or bitterness or as a victim after his brothers sold him into slavery.

For any person to be successful, they have to use adversaries and challenges to make themselves stronger and wiser. The adversaries could be other humans, situations, policies, discrimination, or any other thing. Observe the impure thoughts and challenges and work on overcoming them. These challenges do not have to be people but instead can be goals or fears to defeat or bringing some positive changes to our lifestyle. Usually, we already have adversaries to beat, but before, we used to see them as a misfortune that we succumb to or that break us or victimize us. Now change your perspective about all these situations and try to find the good in them and how each can make you stronger and wiser.

See fear, anxiety, perturbations, and other temporary negative thoughts as your friends that came to point out where you need to purify yourself from illusions. They will make you strong and solid spiritually. Look at them and immediately point out the lessons and advantages they came to teach you.

I Know So Many Josephs

Rumi talked about him in his poems,
But I, too, know so many Josephs,
The Joseph who was sexually abused as a child
But grew up to be king of the news, TV shows, and Hollywood.
Yes, I know so many Josephs.
The Joseph who was abandoned as a child
But grew up to change the world.
I know a Joseph who was a child soldier
And grew up to change the world with his music.
I know Josephs who failed in life many times
But made a comeback that blew our minds.
I know a Joseph who grew up in foster homes,
Who grew up to enlighten so many lives.
I know Josephs who are from broken homes
Who grew up to write life-changing books.
You know a Joseph in your life.
Or you are the Joseph.
You, the one who declared, "You can hurt my body but never my soul."
You, the one who said to others, "You are my past. I forgive you all."
You, the one who declared, "I will rise up after the fall."
You, the one who declared, "I will not be enslaved by hate and hurt."
You, the one who declared, "Whatever you do, I will love you back."
You are the alchemist who transmutes

The failure to success,
The wars to peace.
You are the Joseph.
You are the Joseph that inspires my life.

Bad Relationship Clinging

Many of us waste our time and energy clinging to bad relationships with people who do not treat us with respect and those who take advantage of us. When we get courageous enough to walk away from a bad relationship, we give a chance for good people to come into our lives. Do not be afraid to walk away from people who don't deserve your friendship. The people you allow to come close to you can significantly impact your life, depending on the level of your consciousness or enlightenment. The more conscious you are, the more you will be able to use their weaknesses for your enlightenment. Walk away from people with negative energy as soon as you can. Avoid them like a plague, and in the meantime, use their low energy as an alarm that wakes you up to enlightenment.

Even the strongest character and the most intelligent are weakened by negative energy in their immediate environment if they do know how to transmute all interactions to their own benefit. But even these transmutations take away the time we could have used to do other good things or just enjoy our lives. You should learn and grow from every experience but don't waste your life living with such people just to learn lessons.

The negative energies are brought about by people closest to you—spouse, friends, family, neighbors, coworkers, and the other people you interact with daily. Countless talents and great minds have been laid to waste by these negative interactions. Just like most murders are committed by the people close to each other or who know each other, the culprits for wastage of these talents are the people close them.

Most of these culprits are not even aware that they carry this life-wasting energy. For most, the environment they grew up in passed on this energy to them, and they have no knowledge of how to get rid of it. If they knew better, they would have lived and acted better. They did not deliberately choose these negative behaviors and emotions. Hence, we should offer them complete forgiveness but also keep our interactions with them to a bare minimum. Love them all, for they are children of God. They are here to teach us a great lesson and make us better people. Don't waste even a minute of your life thinking that they are targeting you personally; they are just being who they are, and you should be who you are and use the experience to your advantage. That way, you will not miss out on life. Do not blame yourself and certainly do not blame them.

Can you complain about why the earth does not have two suns? Can you complain about why we have gravity on earth? Or can you complain about the movements of our stars and galaxies? As well, how can you complain about the actions and opinions of others? They are as much a part of our universe as the sun and the earth. We just have to accept and love them unconditionally, as much as we accept our universe and the different elements in it unconditionally.

Why should you expect anybody to apologize for the type of life they chose? They are being who they are, the egoistic identity they assumed out of ignorance. I accept everybody as they are and focus on their good nature, not their weaknesses. I know deep inside there is a part of me that is untouchable, pristine, and sinless. It's up to each one of us to manifest its qualities. It is a choice. You choose: love or hate, reality or illusion, happiness or sadness, peace or war, good health or bad health. Similarly, you can choose to use your tongue to bless someone or hurt someone.

If only people opened their eyes to the low and negative energies that are eating away their lives and slowly killing them. If they knew, they would drop everything and live the enlightened life of true happiness and contentment. They would become the best in whatever they do and reach their true potential.

Enoch Mamo

Life as a Canvas

Let's look at our lives
Like a piece of canvas,
And we were each handed only a piece
To record all our lives' emotions.

You are provided with all the colors in spray bottles.
You are also provided with acids in similar containers.
On your happy days, you spray the canvas with colors to express your joys,
And on your bad days, you spray with acid that leaves the canvas with holes.

Just like the spray bottles, your life is in your hands.
Imagine yourself standing in front of God
And explaining to him what you did with your canvas.
Is it full of holes or it is covered with colors?

4

The Present Moment

Appreciating and Living in the Now

The present moment is the most precious gift we have. That is why we call it "present." It is the only thing certain and eternal. It can never get better than this, so make the best of it. Everything comes and goes, including you. Do not live for tomorrow and do not live in the past; they are both equally life wasting. This is your time, and tomorrow will be another person's time. If you are dreaming of writing great poems, write them now. There is no time that is greater or more perfect than now. Sing the song in your heart now. Now is the best time to have supreme confidence, happiness, health, abundance, and other amazing things in life. Now is the best time to live that life you always dreamt of. Now you are living your dream, with all its imperfections. Living your dream does not mean a perfect life with no challenges. You are given this blessing of the present moment to do extraordinary things and live your life fully. Life does not need preparation, and life does not need a rehearsal.

The tragedy of life is living your life and wasting it in perpetual waiting, waiting to do this and waiting to do that. You think you have the time, and you think you control what happens the next moment or day. The best poems are written now. You will never prepare enough. Preparation is the illusion of the ego that wastes life. There is no better time to share or publish your poems and essays than now. The infinite intelligence in you does not need any preparation or readiness. You have all you need already; all you are required to do is to start living your life this very second without worrying about the future or regretting the past. Do not put off any projects or dreams for any reason.

The life you have now is precious. Do not let anybody or any events steal away your life or time. The thief is the egoistic mind that says tomorrow is a better day to start living your dream. Do all you can today. The best poems are written today, and the best life is now. That image you have in your mind of the good life, live it now.

You are great now, more than you will ever be great at any time in the future. Every minute you have now, write the greatest poems or do those amazing things you have always dreamt of doing. You can never get more inspired or enlightened than you are already now. Take a few seconds and think of all you have done in life: your toils, years in school, aspirations, and dreams to become this person you are now. You didn't get here by mistake or chance, but the universe conspired to get you here in this position and in this moment. It is like you are travelling on a bus, and the driver tells you that you have already arrived when you thought that there was more distance to go. Do you insist on going beyond your destination just because you didn't expect to arrive so soon? Do not be fooled by the promise of tomorrow when you will be writing more beautiful and inspiring poems; that is just an illusion that killed many people before they could sing the song in their hearts. You have already wasted many years because of the illusions of a better tomorrow. The good you hope to see tomorrow is an illusion and a bad dream that is wasting away your life. Few things are more sinful than living in expectation of a better tomorrow by wasting today. A good life is realizing the preciousness of the present moment. The enlightened moment is with you now, and the insightful and beautiful poems are with you now. There is no another time or moment that you will write a better poem. Overcome the illusion of time that you will write a better or greater inspired poem tomorrow or in the future. Do not wait for that perfect moment when everything will come together for you to achieve great things or live a great life.

The ego says that today is not the best time to write your poems or do other things. It will persuade you to do it tomorrow or next week, next month, or next year when you are more peaceful, calm, and enlightened. It will urge you to read more books, learn more vocabularies, get married, be in a better state of joy and confidence, or get a better job. Once you fulfill all these, only then will it be the right time for you to write your book or poems. I know for certain that day will never come. That day doesn't even exist. The ego will always give you an excuse to postpone your life, happiness, health, writing poems or essays, or doing other things.

At some point in life, you feel tired or uncomfortable or lazy about taking action that goes toward fulfilling your dreams. This feeling is created by the egoistic mind that tells you this is not the right time or place to work on your dream. The ego by its intense and habitual urging will make you feel uncomfortable or even make you feel sick to prevent you from enjoying your life now. Do not give the ego the power to control your life and waste it. Once you observe and realize the lies, the ego will disappear.

The best action is to observe the feeling and ignore the ego and go ahead and do whatever you were supposed to do. Victory begins the moment you realize that the moment has already arrived, and it is now or never. This is the best moment to take action and work on your dreams. You cannot arrive at the Olympics and say you want more days to train; the games will go on without you. That is the same in life. It will go on without you, whether you decide to make your contributions or not. Do not hold back your talent; the world is waiting to hear your story. Express yourself in whatever form you desire and leave tomorrow for the next generation to play their part. You are already at the Olympics. Don't retreat. When you work out in a gym to grow your muscles, you pick up the weight that stresses them. Likewise, the moment you overcome that resistance and work on your dream, that is when you are in an excellent position to fulfill your heavenly purpose. Celebrate that moment you resisted procrastination.

Infinite intelligence never deserts you, and your peace and joy never desert you. It is only the ego that created these feelings and veils. The ego is not you. The ego disappears like darkness disappears when you put on the light. You do not even have to fight the ego, as you cannot fight darkness. It is an illusion that momentarily tricks you into feeling that it is you.

These practices will become sweeter as you overcome greater challenges. These moments of eternal personal victory came in the times you decided to quit smoking, the times you decided to work on your dreams, the times you decided to make peace, the times you decided to exercise, the times you decided to improve and change your diet, the times you decided to quit drugs or alcohol, the times you decided to quite bad relationships, the times you decided to improve your relationships, the times you decided to do your homework, the times you decided to work on those great ideas you had been putting away, the times you decided to follow your heart, the times you decided to abandon bad habits and to become a better you.

Let the ego not fool you into thinking that there is always a next moment or future time to take that important step. Let the ego not fool you into thinking that this is easy, and you will do it next time. Let the ego not fool you by making you feel at ease and comfortable postponing your life. The best time to take those actions is now. This is the most important time, and it is the most valuable resource you have in this world. Don't be fooled by tomorrow, for tomorrow is not guaranteed. The now is a powerful tool that dissolves all illusions, as there is no seeking for fulfillment in the future, and there is no living in the past.

I was inspired by the Rio Olympics song that says, "I am unstoppable today." It is not I am unstoppable forever, or tomorrow, or in the future. That is a big message that describes the theme at any

Olympics, and that is how we should live our lives. It is today or the present time that is important. We complicate our lives by worrying about the future or the long term. Who gave you the guarantee of reaching that future? Why should you waste the present by worrying about the future? If you cannot enjoy the present time, then you will also worry if that future comes, because you will be worried about another coming future and other things.

When you are at the battlefront facing your enemies, you cannot ask for time off because you are not prepared enough, or because you don't have the right guns or equipment, or the weather is not nice, or you are not feeling well, or you are not skilled enough, or any other reason. You fight or you die. In life, it is the same. You accept your lot and live a fulfilled life according to nature or you die psychological or even physical death because you refused to accept your lot.

Acceptance of Infinite Intelligence

All these great men and women accepted their gifts/treasures, talents, and resources within to change the world in their respective fields, such as inventions, arts, scientific discoveries, entrepreneurship, political movements, and philosophical, spiritual, and literary writings. The knife never says to you, "I will chop only tomatoes or onions." You decide what you want to chop, and the knife can never refuse to do its job. The infinite intelligence will never fail to do its job in whatever fields you choose to follow. Intuitions, talents, and ideas will not fail to come or flow out. It is your mental thoughts about their limitations that veil them or prevent them from coming out. If you think of them as infinite and accept and recognize these gifts/treasures now, they will come out or flow out infinitely, every second and minute of your life, ignore the wandering away of the mind into thoughts of scarcity.

The logo of Nike, "Just do it," applies to faith. When you think of doing something, do not doubt where those skills, ideas, intuitions, or talents will come from; just do it. Depend on the preparedness of the infinite intelligence. It is always in you, ready and prepared for your unlocking or tapping. The knife is ready to chop whatever foodstuffs you put on the chopping board, so stop doubting or asking the knife if it is ready. Just do it. Why wait? Start using it now.

Take this acceptance, recognition, faith of the infinitely abundant wealth, health, talent, skill, intelligence, and other blessings as your eternal blessing or part of your nature now. You need no struggles, purifications, preconditions, time, lifestyle changes, or changes in your circumstances or conditions. First accept this truth in you now, and then other changes will come to you naturally. The unacceptance of the present moment will only perpetuate your problems through continuous seeking or searching or working hard to unlock these infinite resources or blessings or grace within you. You see, you already have been experiencing the power and miracles of infinite intelligence by unconsciously creating a bad life for yourself in the past; now use it to create a good life for yourself and others. You just have to accept the power of infinite intelligence and its infinite blessings now, in this very moment. It is the illusion of needing more time that is preventing you from unlocking or tapping into this infinite intelligence, power, and abundance. How many more days or years will you continue withholding these infinite powers and blessings? Didn't you already waste many years in the past withholding them and living in scarcity, confusion, poverty, bad heath, failures, and discontentment? How long will you postpone your happiness, success, wealth, peace, good health, confidence, courage, power, talents, skills, and many other abundant blessings? Accept them now. Ignore the illusion of needing more time.

This simple ignorance of the illusion of needing more time will powerfully and instantly wipe out all the other illusions. You will kill all the other illusions with one stone, because all the other illusions live or thrive in the thoughts of past or the future. Past—in form of past identities and opinions of seeing yourself as poor, scarce, unskilled, untalented unintelligent, unblessed, limited, discontented, a failure, and all other negative thoughts or self-images created by the ego. Future—because the ego tells you that your salvation will come in the future after you accomplish something great; you will be happy, peaceful, confident, talented, skilled, wealthy, abundant, intelligent, or blessed in the future. The ego promises you a mirage of a beautiful and abundant future, hence wastes the now, which is the only power you have in this world to access the infinite intelligence within. If you are robbed of the only power you have, then you are left with nothing, all because you ignored or did not accept the only true and real power you have in this world, which is the present moment or the now.

Acceptance of the blessings now will change your life beyond your understanding. Miracles and infinite intelligence and abundance will then work through you. Just realize this is the only powerful tool to change or manifest anything in your life. Don't put down this tool. Putting down this tool means you are missing out on true life and living in an illusion of powerlessness, eternal scarcity, failure, and discontentment. How can you search for power, abundance, success, peace, love, and other blessings when you have ignored or thrown away the only tool that enables their manifestation? You can feel or experience any of them only in the present moment. How can you search for life by wasting life (the present moment)? All the fears, worry, anxiety, weaknesses, scarcity, poverty, sickness, perturbation, doubt, and confusion come because you are wasting or have ignored your present moment or the now. All those negative emotions and experiences indicate this wastage of the present moment. Consciously observe what you are feeling *now*.

The power of the present moment or the now does not need any external conditions, preconditions, or perfections; the power itself comes by seeking none of them, as they just create veils that make it impossible for you to access the power of now and infinite intelligence. Living in the present moment means you live in faith; you trust the presence of infinite blessings and resources within you now.

Today Is "The Best Day of My Life"

"Today is the best day of my life." When I was writing those words in my diary, I wondered if it really was the best day of my life. I asked myself if there were other days I recorded in the past as my best days. I asked myself if I was betraying or reducing the importance of other good things that I received in the past, or if I was less grateful or appreciative of past achievements and good days.

Then I realized that comparing the past "good days" with the now or the happiness I am feeling today, these two comparisons were totally wrong. It is like comparing the dead with the alive; the past is dead. What significance does the past's best days have now? Whether you did something good or bad, those past days are gone, and those feelings and moments are gone. The present is alive, and it is the most real and powerful moment in which I am feeling these emotions. I am connected with or in tune with the infinite intelligence now. This connection can happen only in the now.

The past and the future are illusions of time; they don't exist for me. Therefore, the present is the only time or day that exists and is real and alive. I cannot compare the dead with the alive. The present time or the now is the best time of my life always and has no comparisons. I asked myself, which one is more influential, the dead Steve Jobs or the alive mosquitos that are biting me now? The alive mosquito is more influential than the dead Steve Jobs in this present moment or the now. The mosquito is biting me and making me move or act right now, and the dead Steve Jobs can do nothing to anyone in this present moment. That is how powerful living in the present means. It is the only time where you can be influential or powerful and move, act, talk, feel, love, and do many other things.

Before his death, Steve Jobs was one of the most powerful human beings on this earth. Now, the weakest and tiniest living thing like a mosquito is more powerful and influential than Steve Jobs, only because the mosquito is alive now. You have in your hands the most powerful, most real, most valuable, and most alive period in your life.

It is the present moment. You are alive now. It is the only time you can do anything in this world and with your life. The past and the future do not matter; they are nothing and are not important at all.

Today is the best day of your life, simply because it the only day you are alive. Tomorrow is not guaranteed, and you cannot live in the past. So, why are you worried about the future, whether you will be successful, powerful, wealthy, influential, or happy? Enjoy and value the present moment and the power you have now. Tomorrow or in the future, the mosquito will be more powerful or influential than you, if you are dead. All you have and all you are, is in the present moment, the now. All that matter is what you do or feel now. What you did or felt in the past does not matter. As well, what you will do and feel in the future does not matter. The past is dead, and the future is not yet real.

Checking the Quality of Your Present Moment

You can look at the present moment or the now as a state of mind to help you examine whether you are enjoying the present moment or wasting it. Reflect on your thoughts and self-image in the present moment. Do you see yourself as complete or incomplete? As contented or discontented? As healthy or unhealthy? As abundant or poor? As courageous or a coward? As strong or weak? As intelligent or a fool? As enlightened or unenlightened? As talented or not talented? As useful or unimportant? As happy or not happy? As pure or sinful? As powerful or powerless? As a victim or a victor? As forgiving or vengeful? As unlucky or lucky? As grateful or ungrateful? As suffering or celebrating life? As confident or not confident? As a winner or a loser? As peaceful or perturbed? As relaxed or tense? As beautiful or ugly? As full of self-doubt or full of self-belief? As loving or unloving? As generous or selfish? Mature or immature? Fast or slow? Witty or unwitty? As having a purpose in life or not having a purpose in life? As in the process of discovering the meaning of your life or as someone who has discovered the meaning of his/her life?

How you see yourself now determines the quality of your present moment and your reality. If you have a positive self-image, then you are enjoying the present moment, which will in turn create more joyful realities. This exercise collapses the illusion of time if you simply focus on the present moment rather than judging your past or worrying about the future.

Means and Waste

It is always a good practice to ask yourself whether you are using the present moment as a means to achieve something greater in the future. Are you only focused on the future and seeing your present as just a stepping-stone for the future happiness? Are you abandoning your present happiness in hope of getting happy in the future? Are you looking at the present as a bad time to tolerate? Are you saying to yourself, "I am suffering now for a better future"? I have seen people who wasted the best years of their life in anticipation and preparation for a better or a happy future. Not even a lifetime of prayer can bring back the years they wasted. They will only look back in regret at the wasted years and youth. Live a happy and a good life now, and it will lead you to more happiness and a good life later. Live a miserable and bad life now, and it will lead you to more misery and a bad life later.

The future is not guaranteed. Cherish the present time to have a brighter future. Avoid the habit of sticking your neck out to look for the future and miss seeing the beauty of the present time that is literally a gift right in front of you. Do not hold back any joy for the sake of the illusory brighter future. This moment is eternal. Do not use the present moment as a means to an end. The present moment is the beginning and the end. It is the alpha and the omega. Do not hold back your life.

Our Time Is More Important Than Our Task

Anything you do, whether it is good or bad, big or small, will not add a single day to your life.

The most important thing is the day itself rather than the activity. When you are aware of the importance of the day or value the present time, you will spend it wisely and on important things.

One of the biggest mistakes we make is to think that whatever we are doing is very important, and hence we feel tense, confused, and sometimes intimidated by the task that we have in our hands. Part of this is largely because we had the wrong priority regarding what is important. The most important thing is not even the work that we are doing or what we are doing; it is our time (our life). We are doing whatever we are doing probably for money, but the most important thing is we are giving away a piece of our life to these tasks. The job can change, or we can get a better one, the money can be lost, or we can get more, but the time we spend can never be regained. It is a piece of our life gone, a piece of our youth, a piece of our energy, a piece of our precious time. These are the things that are more important. At any work, we should remember what is important and derive the maximum joy from what we are doing. The work that we are doing or will be doing should be judged based on whether we are enjoying what we are doing or if we are doing it just for the money. Ask yourself if this is the job where you want to spend your precious life or your last days on this earth. Ask yourself what you are sacrificing that job or career for. Ask yourself hard questions and find the answers now to live a happy and healthy life. Do not cover up your present with lies and procrastinations. Be true to yourself.

Abusing your body, health, or dignity for any kind of financial gain or leisure is a waste of life. Those are the most valuable things you own that cannot be compared to anything external, and yet you give them away for frivolous and slavish external things. True gain, whether financial or happiness, does not require the abuse or sacrifice of your integrity or health. You should always be careful and pay attention to what you are giving in exchange for the wages or salaries you get at work. Don't sell your body to buy clothes and don't lose your health at work or you will spend your earnings on treatments.

Be in charge of your own kingdom first, and the rest will follow. Be loyal and protect your principles and philosophies with your life each day. The future and the past don't matter. Live your present supremely. That is all you really own. Do not give away your peace of mind, respect, health, dignity, and confidence to get money, a job, a promotion, leisure, friendship, or any other favors. You gain nothing by allowing fear, worry, sickness, perturbation, and anxiety to take over your life.

DECISION MAKING PROCESS

What is decision making? How do you make decision from a position of strength rather than weakness? In what state of mind should you be now, in order to make the right decision? While also making sure you don't waste your present moment in negative thoughts and emotions of frustrations, weakness, confusion, uncertainty, fear, worry and anxiety that makes decision making difficult?

Starting point, realize that all you have and all you ever have is this present moment, it's the only and most powerful and most valuable treasure that the ego's illusion can take away from you. And it has taken away this power from you, if you start feeling or experiencing negative thoughts and emotions. Remember, that was the ego's main goal, to steal away or waste your present moment, and once it has done that, you are left in a position of weakness and all the negative thoughts or emotions overwhelm your hours and days with frustration, fear, complexity, uneasiness, perturbation etc. Here, you are guaranteed to make the wrong decision and regret it later, because you are motivated and driven by fear, weakness and guilt etc. Your perception of how you look at things or your current situation is shaped by those negative emotions and thoughts. Regrets, come when you make a decision from a position of weakness as you are mentally and emotionally under duress. Why do you put yourself through this? Because someone made you feel guilty, remorseful or made you feel bad through negative comments or suggestions, or, these guilts and regrets were produced by your own negative thoughts or opinions about yourself. Therefore, remind yourself first, not to allow those negative thoughts/emotions/illusions to steal away your present moment/power/peace of mind/positive self-esteem that helps you make the right decision. Remind yourself, you have all these within you already now and the power of infinite intelligence that guides you in making the right decision. This faith will be the building blocks in your creation in the invisible world. So here, you are operating from a position of power, wisdom, peace, right-mindedness, strength, love, confidence and courage.

Do not think or say "the infinite intelligence will give me the right decision in due time" do not wait, consciously think and formulate your best options. There is no better or more suitable time to make that decision outside the present moment or the NOW. The ego tries to steal away your present moment by asking you to wait for a better time, a calmer or perfectly peaceful place or space or environment to make that decision, this will in fact increase your anxiety. There is no more perfect environment, peace of calmer place than within you, and you will never get them from external environment but only within, don't try to find them outside, those are wasteful egoistic thoughts that are trying to find peace and strength from without. Also, the search for these external conditions, means you are also wasting your present moment and confirming the lack of those things within you now.

When you say, "the decision is complex, tough or frustrating etc. then you are saying I am weak to make the right decision and also you are creating in your invisible world these same negative realities of being overwhelmed by those decisions. You are showing your lack of faith in infinite intelligence (God) and giving the power to illusions or the situations. That is making you see all your options as stressful with no possible good outcome. You don't see a win-win, but only win-loss, loss-loss (damn if you do it and damn if you don't), this is because you already damned your present moment. So, what do you expect? You see what happens when you operate from a position of weakness? You cannot create pleasant or good decision or future from unpleasant or bad present moment. You will reap what you sow. Use the most powerful tool of the present moment for your decision making.

You have to step back, be still and observe who is making the decision now (your self-image or state of mind), is it the weak you or the strong you? When you are wise to know that there is nothing greater for you to lose other than this present moment, then you will have true independence and wisdom to make the right decision.

Wasting Your Life Pleasing Others

A great number of people waste their lives trying to make everybody else happy. This attempt will always end up in failure. The people who are fooled by this life- and energy-wasting endeavor do it for a selfish reason of trying to get others like them. But what they are actually doing makes others despise them. Nobody likes and respects the "yes" characters. They are considered as easygoing and wishy-washy who have no personal principles.

People admire someone who has principles and is not afraid to say no or express their true feelings when necessary. You have to learn to say no in your everyday interactions with people. You have to congratulate yourself for saying no at the end of each day or week. It is the no that makes others respect and admire you. The more no's you say, the more honor you get. This is not just for the sake of defiance, but it is a call for a true self-expression. We are attracted to people who say no because they have principles and have the confidence and courage to express their feelings. You say no whenever you do not feel good about something or your intuition alerts you. The habit will take some time to become part of your nature, but if you keep exercising on small things in life, that will in turn build your confidence to say no to bigger requests. Before you know it, the no will come out automatically without you even noticing it, but in the beginning, you have to make deliberate efforts. Do not get frustrated if you fail to adapt to the new habit right away. Give yourself some time and keep practicing.

Saying no should not make you feel guilty; instead, it is saying yes to everything that should make you feel guilty. Saying no, for the right reasons reveals courage and principles. It grows your confidence and prevents unnecessary stresses in life.

Mr. Yes characters are weak in nature and will readily give away their money, property, or time and effort to others not because they are good people but because they are eager to please others at whatever cost. They do not have good self-esteem and thus seek others' approval to feel worthy. Mr. Yes characters believe their worthiness comes from without but not within. They feel good about themselves only when people say good things about them. They have the impossible mission of trying to please everyone in their lives, and they abandon their own happiness in the process. To remove these diseases, do not focus on the past. It will take a lifetime or more to analyze the past mistakes where you tried to please someone even though the act betrayed all your principles and beliefs. Instead you should focus on the present in order to develop and strengthen your core principles and values, which will guide your response in all circumstances.

Your attempt to please others and look like others withdraws a large amount of power from your life and kills your creativity and intuitions. You should waste no energy and time to become another. And the only way you can know who you are is by removing and abandoning who you are not, and the real you will shine through.

Whenever you say 'yes' all the time, remember you are not being nice, but instead it shows cowardice in many instances. In addition to your time and energy, in a lot of cases it also means you are giving away your respect, principles, and confidence. Saying no, doesn't mean you are a bad or mean person. It proves honor and respect. It will also make the other person better because they will be reasonable in their demands next time.

I have observed people who have made a career for themselves by saying no, as judges on reality television. They are admired and worshiped for their true self-expression or intuitions. You will never get anywhere in life by saying 'yes' all the time.

The nice guy or Mr. 'Yes' label is an umbrella under which most fearful people live. If you take off the mask, you will find a mortally fearful and timid individual filled with rage and regrets because of their inability to express themselves. How lucky are you if people call you a bad person because you refused to abandon your principles and intuitions, it means people respect you. The nice person is one who seeks pity rather than demanding respect from others. The nice person has weak principles, thus readily follows the opinions of others without challenging them. They believe having their own opinion means offending others, so they have to adopt other people's opinions and beliefs to maintain the false peace.

How Do You Avoid or Get Rid of Mr. Yes?

How do you avoid becoming Mr. Yes, the pleasing character or the fake self? I wrote some questions that can help you examine your motivations and actions. Ask yourself the following questions:

- What makes me happy or makes me feel good about myself? Is it saying yes to others by abandoning my own happiness, intuitions, principles, beliefs, duties, goals, and missions?
- What creates my self-worth or self-esteem? Is it from within or without?
- How can I examine if I am doing things just to appease others or to get the label of Mr. Yes?
- What are the warning signs of Mr. Yes actions?
- How do I feel right now? How do I see myself now? How did I see myself in the past? And what is the projection of

my future self-image? What kind of imagination do I have regarding my future self-esteem?

- What is the quality of my present moment?
- Is it my own opinion and self-image of seeing myself as Mr. 'Yes' that is creating my reality?
- Does the past have power to influence my present or my future?
- Which one do I consider most powerful—my present, future, or past?
- What makes my present, future, or past most powerful? Which one of them created my present reality of how I see myself?
- Is how I see myself now a result of my own opinion or others' opinions?

The most powerful and the most real self-image is the one you are creating right now, consciously or intentionally, in this present moment, whether the self-image you choose is positive or negative. Either one of them will form your reality.

Sometimes the ego can come up with self-doubting questions or thoughts, such as:

- My past self-image is the only real me I know.
- My past self-image is too difficult to change. That is how people know me and have known me all my life.
- Creating a new self-image means creating a fake me. It feels like I am betraying my old identity.
- Creating a new self-image may offend my friends, family, and other people I know.
- The new self-image is hard to maintain. I will go back to my old self or self-image pretty soon.
- Creating a new self-image will make me look strange or crazy.

You have to ask yourself, which of the two self-images you value more, your past self-image created unconsciously by your opinion and others' opinions or your self-image created consciously by you in the present moment?

Consciously creating a positive self-image in the present moment, valuing it, and maintaining it simply through focusing on how you see yourself in the present moment will make you a master of your reality and your world. On the other hand, sticking to your past self-image created unconsciously by yourself and others' opinions will make you a slave of the past and others' opinions.

When you choose your new self-image, you are choosing a lifetime of guaranteed happiness, abundance, strength, peace of mind, health, and wealth. On the other hand, when you choose to stick to your past negative self-image, you are choosing a lifetime full of perturbations, weakness, scarcity, sadness, sickness, and discontentment every time you perceive that someone has unfavorable opinion of you. The constant search for others' approval will make you feel scarcity or lacking a good self-image. The stress that comes because of all these bad feelings will end up making you sick and less able to grow your earthly health and wealth.

You should also ask yourself what motivates your actions or why you do what you do now.

- Is it because you want to create or maintain a positive self-image in people's minds, or are you acting in accordance with your principles and beliefs?
- Is the good you do good for you and other people?
- Where are your good deeds coming from? Are they from abandoning your principles, beliefs, and intuitions? This means your good deeds are coming from a position of weakness and negative self-image.
- Are your good deeds coming from your intuitions, beliefs, and principles? This means your good deeds are coming from a position of strength and positive self-image.

Slave of Good Deeds

If someone did something good for you, do not be enslaved by those deeds such that you in exchange give away your dignity and integrity to make them feel important and have pity on you. That would be selling your soul to the devil. If you are giving away any of those things, it means you are being exploited and enslaved either consciously or unconsciously. Appreciate and recognize the good act or return the favor if possible. Do not feel forever indebted for the good deeds; your life or soul should not be sold or exchanged for frivolous favors. If a person keeps mentioning to you the favors they did for you to make you submissive and feel inferior, then it is time for you to move away from that individual as soon as possible because this is a form of emotional abuse and torment.

The Moon Staring at Me

I am seated outside, and the moon is bright and staring at me.
I don't know if she wants to say something.
She looks so close and warms my heart with her brightness.
Earlier today, I saw her out before even the sun went home.
I don't know if she had an early date or she wanted to give the sun company.
I believe they are still dating and their love is just as strong.
Or Is she tired of the distant relationship and wants to melt into his arms?
What does she have to say about our visit to her place?
Was she very welcoming or did she see us as intruders?
I see and admire her from afar.
I see the faint outline of the craters in her belly.
Can she see mine? She is just so lovely.
I am awed by her beauty.
I am awed by her calm demeanor.
In her presence, I am filled with joy.

I forget everything and stared back at her for long.

She just wants to be quiet today and wants me to learn something from her silence.

I can feel her warmth on a cold night.

I thank her silently. I hope she hears my gratitude.

How lucky I am to experience this beauty.

She wants to give me company like she has for billions of other beings.

But tonight, I feel like she chose me for a conversation.

I am grateful beyond words and want to just sit and enjoy the moment.

She is just covered by the sky, is that her blanket? I think that is a way for her saying goodbye.

She is going to sleep, and I wished her a good night.

5

Fear and Worry

Living with Fear and Worry

We are so used to living in worry that we think there is no any other way of living. Many of us are resigned to the false fact that to live is to worry. There is worry mongering and profiting by big businesses. These are done through endless campaigns to make us worry about our retirement, our investments and savings, our insurance policies, our mortgages, our careers, our loans, our children, our aging, our health, our eating habits, our politics, wars and trades.

You close one hole of worry; another comes up simultaneously. You are told, "You are good or covered here but not there." You spend all your life dealing with one worry after another. You are taught to believe that it is how life is. We try to normalize the abnormal. Why all these worries to live and die? You will still live and die, with or without the worry. In between, it matters how you live your life.

Why are we filled with worry and doubt in spite of the power of the infinite intelligence within us? It is the doubt that results in all our pain and suffering. Stop being too anxious! Trust in the infinite intelligence within you that has all the answers, and you will discover amazing strength and abundance within that will overcome all your worries.

What is all this fear of hunger? Trust in God, and what you

are lacking will come to you. Isn't it surprising that the people who are worried most about their future, financial security, and career are the ones who end up with a miserable future, with poverty and a mediocre career? That comes from loss of trust in the infinite intelligence within you to provide you with a comfortable life. Your worry and anxiety bring upon the same things you feared.

A lot of our troubles or the failures to reach our goals are because we don't understand the law of the universe, and therefore we doubt the very law that rules the universe, which is we get out of the universe what we put in. All religious books, prophets, sages, and philosophers have stated that same simple fact. You have to trust in this law. Whatever you thought of or focused on will definitely come true. This law is so simple, and yet we complicate our lives by doubting or ignoring this fact.

Your imagination creates your world. You are imagining even the times when you think you are not imagining. You are imagining all the time. A lot of people imagine unconsciously and create what they fear. The wise imagine consciously and create what they want: what type of day they want, what type of interaction they want to have, what kind of life they want to have, and so on. Choose wisely what you imagine.

Anxiety/Worry/Fear as Creations in an Invisible World

The illusions of worry, fear, and anxiety are all forms of creation in the invisible world (first creation), which is the most powerful stage of creation and the most important because it is happening now in the present moment and determines your visible reality or outcome. Thoughts of fear, worry, and anxiety about your future or what is going to happen to you or those around you wastes your present moment, even though those things have not happened yet. These negative emotions and thoughts are the first stage of creation in the invisible world (you already feel as though those things have already happened or are real). Eventually your dwelling thought or faith will type those messages or orders onto your subconscious mind, which will faithfully bring those thoughts into your visible reality. These fears will create your reality and will come to pass, regardless of how remote or improbable those events and happenings are in normal life. All the forces of the universe will come together perfectly to make your fears come true (this is the opposite of manifesting thoughts of astronomical or improbable success). Faith knows no impossibility or improbability; that is why you see astronomical or astonishing success or failure, wealth or poverty, health or sickness. All of them have equal power to create our reality in the visible world. For simplification, let us call these two kinds of faiths as the positive/good faith and the other as negative/bad faith. The good faith, emanating from positive thoughts of success, abundance, good health, and so on will lead you to living in the present moment since you are experiencing calmness, peace of mind, reassurance, confidence, ease, tranquility, serenity, contentment, comfort, solace, relief, and so on. The bad faith will make you experience the opposite of those feelings and experiences. You are experiencing all the good vibes now, and eventually your invisible world will create your visible world; they will come to pass. So, does it even matter what you will create eventually in your visible world or reality in the end? Is it difficult for you to understand why you should choose the good faith or thoughts of abundance and success or to believe only good things will happen to you and for you and the people around you? What will you lose by choosing the good faith? You will only lose thoughts and emotions of fear, worry, and anxiety. The good and the bad faith will give you completely opposite present moments and eventually opposite outcomes or external realities. If you look at your life as a journey, which of the two paths would you like to take? Will you choose a journey of pain, fear, perturbation, and other miseries? Does the destination really matter here if the journey is a misery? Why do we choose fear or worry or anticipate bad things happening to us? Most people do not make these choices consciously.

This is lack of right-mindedness, enlightenment, or wisdom. When you choose fear, it means you are confirming or implying that you are powerless and that other people, institutions, and fate determine your destiny. It means you have decided or chosen to create or bring into reality those negative thoughts. At the end, you may say it is meant to happen or expected to happen, or it is meanness of the other people, or it is because of bad institutions or systems, or it is the fault of others, or it is what others told you to fear or expect, or it is what others experienced before you, or it looked like there was no other possible outcome, or you had no choice, it is the culture or tradition, or it is your nature to be fearful and worry. You can attribute to this life-wasting illusion one or more of the above excuses, but nothing can justify it. You see, all those excuses are a way of you saying, "I am justified or right to choose a journey of pain or to waste my present life and moment." While these same thoughts or excuses are powerfully and undeniably creating your visible external reality, in the end, your own thoughts created those realities, not other people or external other forces. The external forces and other people and events were working to bring to pass your dwelling thoughts, whether those thoughts were positive or negative. The creation started in your invisible world. All those people, institutions, and circumstances were working to make your dream come true, or in case of the bad faith, to make your nightmares come true. How do you then blame people, institutions, or events you chose to work for you that are faithfully following your orders, typed messages, and instructions?

When you say, "Infinite intelligence within me is powerful," you are implying or confirming the simple truth and universal law that your dwelling thoughts or faith are powerful enough to create your reality. In other words, your invisible creation is creating your visible world. You are therefore declaring your infinitely abundant power of determining your fate or destiny. You are saying, "What I typed is what I will see on the printout." If you have been making those choices unconsciously, observe and practice consciousness now. If you have been unconsciously making people, institutions, or events work against you, now consciously choose to make them work in your favor or for your good or blessing.

I am not promising that you will not experience fear in the future. I am telling you to treat those thoughts or moments of fear as a temporary wandering away of the mind that you should not dwell on or allow to become your permanent reality or life.

The only impossible thing in this world is trying to make the law of the universe work in reverse by trying to create first the visible and then the invisible world. The ego tries to convince you and make you focus only on the visible world and ignore the more important and powerful invisible world. Focusing only on the visible world will make you impatient, discontented, and unfulfilled as see yourself as a failure or lacking something. Below are some of the reasons why so many people ignore the invisible stage of creation:

- They are used to accepting or believing only what they can see.
- They crave for people's approval, praise, and opinion. They are impatient to prove themselves to others and show them how successful they are, so that other people have to witness their success in the visible world.
- They don't see immediate change in the visible or physical world. They want to see instantly the tower (the physical structure) of their mental drawing.
- Not instantly seeing the creation in the invisible world make them think it does not exist (they seek instant gratification and proof). The invisible stage of creation looks too unreal to them since they cannot see it.
- People cannot see instant visible changes in themselves, around them, and in their conditions or material gain, fame, and recognition, so what others cannot see or value is not important or valuable or true to them.

- They are used to their past self-image, condition, and perspective; hence they overlook, ignore, or cannot see/notice the changes that have started taking place in their visible world. Quickly they lose the small gains or positive changes they made and return to their old identities, circumstances, and perspectives. The past/old life looks too familiar and is easy to continue with.
- They have accepted and are resigned to their past identities, a self-image created by their opinion and opinion of others. They think it is impossible to change, and some are afraid of change.
- Many people have strongly rooted beliefs in their religion, culture, and traditions. So, they are not open to change.
- Some think that enlightenment, wisdom, and right-mindedness, such as my teachings about the invisible stage of creation, are too complicated, and it is difficult to understand and live according to these truths. They think it is difficult to imagine or conceptualize the invisible stage of creation as real.
- Many cannot read and write, cannot access materials that can enlighten them, or are denied access by their governments or other people.
- For some, the daily demands of their life, such as work, leisure, family, friends, and other activities, distract them from seeking right-mindedness, wisdom, and enlightenment.
- Some think they need a special power, faith, discipline, or lifestyle to create in the invisible world.

Whatever reason you give for living an unconscious life, just remember the most natural and easiest way to live a good life is to live according to universal laws or truths. The outcomes are guaranteed and require no sacrifice of your life, time, or energy, as you will start living in the now or the present moment. Many people fail because they are trying to reverse the laws or stages of creation.

Following the correct procedure of creation or the universal laws of creation will save you time and energy because it is the only true path to success.

What you did not create in the invisible world, you cannot and will not see in the visible world. And what you created in the invisible world cannot and will not fail to be created in the visible world (your external reality that can be witnessed or seen by all other people). Both your unconscious and conscious creations in the invisible world will be created in your visible world with equal precision and power.

Most of our frustrations are due to our focus on counting, comparing, and valuing only the external treasures, assets, and successes while we ignore the most important treasures within. When you focus on counting your treasures/blessings within, you are being grateful and creating good things in your invisible world. Always look within with thoughts of love, abundance, peace, good health, and infinite blessings. Your trust in God or infinite intelligence will keep you abundant always.

Counting the treasures within or focusing on the invisible stage of creation (which is faith) is more important than counting the visible/external treasures. Counting the internal treasures within will instantly give you peace of mind, happiness, success, and all other blessings and will lead you to enjoy and live in the present moment or the now. On the other hand, counting the external treasures will arouse in you feelings of scarcity, comparison, worry, anxiety, perturbation, failure, and discontent, because, no matter how big the external treasures you have, you will start comparing yourself to other people and feel less fortunate and successful. You will feel poor even if others think you are rich. You will worry or be anxious that it will be taken from you or stolen or taxed or that whatever you have will lose value over time. But counting your treasures within will give you everlasting happiness, contentment, and abundance. They cannot be taken from you or stolen. The more you value the treasures within, the more trust you have in God or the infinite intelligence within, and the more blessed and successful you are to change your life.

Counting, focusing on, and valuing the external treasures is for those without faith and living in ignorance and eternal discontent, worry, perturbation, and unhappiness. Any fool knows how to count external treasures, but only the wise know how to value and count the treasures within. The sooner you value and start counting the treasures within, the sooner you get infinite blessings, happiness, wealth, wisdom, intuitions, truths, peace of mind, contentment, abundance, and all other blessings you want to manifest in your life. That is, the sooner you put your faith and trust in God (infinite intelligence within) to work, the sooner you start creating your desired manifestations in the invisible world. Get your blessings today. You see, in the world of faith, contentment equals wealth. The greater contentment you have, the greater wealth you have. End your worries, anxiety, discontentment, perturbation, and scarcity now. The person who lives in faith lives in eternal abundance, happiness, and other blessings. When you have this faith, this kind of life, you will start truly loving yourself because of your contentment.

The ego will try to make you doubt or create a veil through thoughts of impatience and anxiety by asking for visible proof (external treasures or manifestations) or by asking you how soon they will be manifested in the visible or external world. We already know the fallacy of this illusion, that all manifestations start with invisible creations and that we cannot reverse the stages of creation by seeing or witnessing first in the visible world. When you fall for this illusion of the ego, you start doubting the manifestation (doubting faith) and feel discontented and impatient. The ego will try to tell you, "See! You are the same person in the same poor condition and circumstances." It will try to tell you change is impossible." Remember to treat all these as a simple and temporary wandering away of the mind. Not choosing or following or recognizing the universal laws of stages of creation will guarantee you a life of scarcity, discontentment, perturbation, and unhappiness. The ego is questioning you just to make you doubt, but it cannot give you the right solution or an answer. It will just create in you a feeling of discontentment and scarcity, which will make your situation worse.

How do you solve this? Count and value your treasures within now, in the present moment. Do treasures within create external wealth? Yes, they can only come from within. You have in the past created external poverty and a miserable life for yourself by not valuing and counting the internal treasures within that can be your proof too. Now start creating internal and external treasures and wealth while truly enjoying your life and the present moment. Believe that you have received all your prayers, desires, and goals now and start counting and valuing your treasures within. Be grateful and enjoy your life. When you accept and recognize your prayers as received, it means you have counted your treasures within, and the thoughts are expression of gratitude.

Sometimes you start feeling impatient about achieving your supreme goals because you tend to overlook or forget the good life you are having now or the positive changes in your life and the negative and painful thoughts and illusions you have overcome or wiped out. The ego veils you from noticing and recognizing these gains or achievements, while they are in fact the most important gains or treasures you can have. But egoistic thoughts of greed and discontentment start saying to you, "Show me the money now." This is the ego's attempt to lead you back to your old life of misery. Be grateful and appreciate what you have achieved. Money and accomplishments will not and cannot give you those gains, blessings, and treasures within. The ego is trying to shift the goal post so as to make you waste your life and the most precious and true gift of life, the present moment.

If you are frustrated, unhappy, depressed, perturbed, or got sick trying to make the world a better place, you are making the world a worse place by contributing to the world those negative emotions and energies. Be happy to make the world a happy place. Be healthy to make the world a healthy place. Empower yourself to empower the world. Be at peace to make the world a peaceful place. Change your life positively to bring a positive change to the world. Respect your intuitions, instincts, and decisions to teach others do the same.

Anxiety as a Result of an Attempt to Control

Sometime, anxiety attacks happen when you are trying to control the uncontrollable. The only thing you can control is your mind and thoughts. You cannot control what other people think or their opinion; that is not your business, and it is their world. In this case, the anxiety came due to the ego's attempt to control another person's world. Focus on your thoughts rather than other people's thoughts. When you are focused on yourself, then you do not give that much significance to the opinions of others, which in turn gives you peace of mind. We can also get anxiety because we worry about the outcome of a job interview, a business deal, or other results. This happens because we give more value to these things than to our peace of mind or health. The worry and anxiety will not help to get you that job or business deal.

Fear That Paralyzed the Hero

Fear has paralyzed many of my otherwise courageous brothers and sisters all over the world. This feeling is unnatural and is not real at all. The ego hijacked the body's natural instinct of keeping itself from physical danger and unnaturally transferred those instincts to other aspects of our lives. Fear has kept us away from enjoying our lives and reaching our full potential.

These are fears of offending others, losing friendships or relationships, losing a job, old age, not having enough savings, not having a financially secure retirement, death or a death in the family, talking to people, sickness, getting or applying for a better job, making mistakes, not having enough, debate, police, authorities, talking to girls, divorce, poverty, marriage, dating, intimacy, sex, religions, quitting drugs or alcohol or smoking, dying poor, losing a pension, losing an investment, changing jobs, changing cities, love, making public speeches, asking for a better pay or treatment at work. The list is almost endless. Why all these fears for this short life?

Do not fear to follow your dreams, do not fear to stand up to injustice, do not fear to express your opinion, do not fear about your future, do not fear about your pension, do not fear about failure, do not fear disease, do not fear poverty, and do not fear death. It is those who fear these things who end up with those problems. If you fear poverty, you will be poor; if you fear death, you will die soon; if you fear disease, you will get sick soon; if you fear failure, you will fail soon; if you fear a bad future, you will have a bad future. Does the fear benefit you at all? It is all an illusion that is wasting your life.

If fear comes to your mind, just recognize it as a wandering of the mind, and it will simply go away. Do not make a big deal of it by judging yourself as a fearful person or someone who cannot control their fears. These fears come to all of us, even to the most courageous and successful; the difference is how we chose to deal with it. If you accept it and recognize it as a lie, then you can use it for enlightenment and to make yourself a better person. If you look at it as something that has taken over your life or if you try to fight it, then it will waste your life, and soon the fear will become a reality in your life. Do not let this lie take over your life. Fear is not natural. It is not in your nature to be fearful of anything.

Fear will only consume your life and make you suffer like Job in the Bible. It is better to remain penniless and fearless than to be fearful with enormous wealth around you. First be the ruler of your own mental kingdom by removing illusions rather than attempting to gain an external kingdom because you will not be able to enjoy it with all these fears you have. The spiritual gains you will have by looking within cannot be compared to any amount of money or wealth.

When you see the fog, do you despair because you think it will never go away? We all know that the fog clears. There is no fog that is permanent, and there are no challenges or problems that are permanent. Why do we then despair in the face of life's challenges that will pass away soon? Why do we forget that this too shall come to pass and will make us stronger? Because of things that will eventually clear away, we get frustrated and paralyzed by fear and confusion, which in turn takes away our ability to find a solution.

Removing Anxiety/Worry

It is one of the life-wasting emotions created by the ego. Even though I knew it was the ego's attempt to fool me into this, and I for sure knew it was an illusion, it came back again and again. That doesn't mean it is a failure on your part or my part to remove the ego, but it is because of our mind's nature to wander away into these illusions. So light up the darkness again and again whenever the illusions come back. Don't try to fight or feel guilty or frustrated about it, for that is what the ego wants. The ego wants to feed on this energy and create this identity of a fighter, a guilty or frustrated person. The ego wants to adopt this new identity. There is nothing to fight, nothing to feel guilty about, and nothing to get frustrated about. Again, how can you fight something that doesn't even exist? The ego's illusion created it, and now the ego wants you to fight this illusion. Two illusions cannot make one reality. It's all the wandering of the mind; realize this, and the ego will disappear. That is the best weapon for the ego. It needs no time or effort, and the ego disappears in no time, just like you switch on a light to lighten up the darkness. The darkness disappears with no fight.

So, do not worry about it coming back again and again because you need no effort or time to fight it again and again. Use those experiences to make you wiser and mentally stronger. You should welcome and accept the dark energy and use it as a fuel to drive your growth and strength. That is going to double the resources at your disposal for your spiritual growth and enlightenment.

6

What Is Poverty?

The Mud Pool

Unconsciously, a lot of people pull each other into the mud.
The mud consists of fear, anger, pain, jealousy, hate,
Revenge, poverty, fights, insults, failures, divorce, and guilt.
They pull each other into this pool of mud.
Faster than any plague this pulling will spread.

Each encounter with a person can get you into the dirt.
You can either catch the disease or avoid the plague.
The choice is yours; the consequences are not.
People do not always get into the mud for malice.
You can get into the mud to please someone.
You can get into the mud because you are too polite.
You can get into the mud just to be a part,
To join the mob mentality and suppress the voice in your heart.
Or you can remain in the mud because that was home in the past;
You are now afraid to have a new start.

The journey out could be slow and long.
The walk could be tough and alone.
But the journey is worth it to regain your throne.

Promise yourself not to get into the mud,
Not for anyone and not for anything.
Instead, you should be part of the healing

Poor Thoughts

Poverty is a life filled with negative emotions and habits like; anger, complaint, bad health, lack of self-respect, regrets, guilt, jealousy, hate, revenge, discontent, ingratitude, sadness, sense of inferiority, laziness, drug abuse, abuse of the body through excessive smoking and drinking, fights, insults, emotional abuse, physical abuse, lack of self-expression and fear of speaking your mind, shyness, waste of time by spending too much time on TV and social media, worry, and lack of spiritual growth and moral principles etc. Poverty is never about money and will never be about lack of money or material possessions. If you are free of those life wasting emotions and habits, you will always live in abundance and joy.

Never Focus on Lack

Never ever think that you don't have what the other person has. Never feel small by looking at the talent, skills, wealth, life style, confidence, courage, joy, intelligence, peace of mind, public speaking skills, or possessions other people have and say to yourself, "If only I had that," or "Oh, I don't have that." You have all those things. There is infinite intelligence and treasures and powers within you. The problem was you never recognized them in yourself, and instead you were recognizing in others what they have already recognized within themselves and manifested for the world to see. You never gave the time to look within, but instead you wasted your resources and blessings by gazing at others' blessings. If you recognize those blessings within you, there is no way in this world that those thoughts will not manifest themselves and become your reality. You can only choose what to think. The consequences are out of your hands. Nothing can stop them from becoming a reality. If you think you don't have something, it is not because you lack it within but because of your very thought of lack, which makes it real.

How we can have everything we need, the world's largest treasures within, and ignore them to beg for worthless pennies? The ones who love themselves least get the least amount of love from the world. The ones who give the least attention and time to themselves get the least attention and time from the world. The ones who think of themselves as poor and unlucky get poverty and scarcity from the world. It all comes from you; nothing comes from outside. The external realities are the manifestation of the realities you created within through the power of your daily habitual thoughts.

God is good all the time, and all the time, God is good.

Rules of life are good all the time, and all the time, the rules of life are good. They never fail, and they are eternally true.

You get from life what you create through your daily thoughts and perceptions. You create good and bad in equal proportion of your thoughts of good or bad. Make your thoughts right; make your life right.

Begging for Favors and Other Things

It is better to sleep hungry or not get that important opportunity than beg for anything from anyone—not from any person in this world.

The act of begging or pleading for something will rob you of your dignity and self-respect. Begging means you are giving away the most precious thing in this world, your dignity and respect. Nothing in the world is worth your dignity and respect. It is like you are giving away a kilo of gold to receive a kilo of worthless sand. The gold is your self-respect and dignity, and the sand is what you are seeking outside.

By begging, I mean you make yourself small and pitiful in front of another person in order to ask for a favor. You feel and make yourself smaller than the other person. When you are used to begging, you will beg for even the things that are rightly yours, and you will always feel needy and scarce. You will forget how to ask for and demand what is your basic right. You will have low-self-esteem and a negative self-image, and you will have no confidence to do anything for yourself. The things you are begging for may change, but your begging will never stop. You have to make a conscious effort to stop this habit. It is not only people who are materially poor who beg but also the people who have material wealth. It is the lack of spiritual wealth that makes people beggars.

You think you can get more pity or sympathy than the beggars I see every day on the street of Addis Ababa? If seeking other people's pity and sympathy makes one rich, these beggars would be billionaires. Your begging, seeking sympathy or favors by making yourself small or a victim, adds more suffering and poverty to your life. You have health, a job, shelter, and skills, and yet you want to compete with the beggars for pity and favors from other people. What will another human being give you that God or the infinite intelligence has not given you already? You may say, "Look at my situation. A good life or abundance is unthinkable or impossible for me to get." Well, if that is what you believe, that is what you will get. How else will you change your situation or circumstance? Your negative thoughts and beliefs are creating your reality. No one else can change them but you since it is all taking place in your mind.

Ingratitude

This begging also means wishing, coveting, or desiring to have someone else's life, skills, wealth, talent, lifestyle, success, careers, looks, confidence, leadership skills, writing skills, and so on. When you do this, it means you are confirming and feeling lack of those things in your life. You are telling yourself, hence your subconscious mind and the universe, that you are ungrateful, limited, poor, incomplete, discontent, and miserable. What is the meaning of being grateful when you harbor all those feelings of lack and discontent? What is the significance of saying thank you at night when your day was filled with thoughts of ungratefulness? Do you say thank you or express gratitude only during those rare moments when you see or experience good things coming your way and spend 99 percent of your time on thoughts of ingratitude and lack?

True gratitude is having thoughts of abundance all the time. Saying thank you once a day or once in a while is not enough. It is insignificant or very little. Thus, you end up getting very little or insignificant blessings or abundance. The more grateful thoughts you have, which are thoughts of abundance, wealth, talent, health, skills, and other good things in life, the more of them you get. The more thoughts of ingratitude or lack you have, the more misfortune, lack, failure, and scarcity you will have in your life. The level of your gratitude determines the level of your abundance, skills, or achievements. Unlock the infinite abundance, intelligence, wealth, treasures, and resources within you through your gratefulness. Stop begging while there are infinite blessings, power, intelligence, and abundance within you. Nobody but you, who is withholding those blessings from you.

Think of all you have as abundant and leverage it. The infinite intelligence will provide you with infinite resources to give you astronomical success and a life of supreme and infinite abundance. Tap into those resources now. They are waiting for you to be unlocked.

Most people want something good to happen so that they can be grateful while ignoring the first stage of creation in the invisible world. This makes them waste the present moment or the now in anticipation and anxiety. But thoughts of abundance and contentment (which means you are grateful now) mean you are living in the present moment or the now. The thoughts of abundance will bring you more abundance, as it is your dwelling thought. Do not wait for manifestations (visible or external reality) but live in faith. Accept and be grateful for the invisible now, as it is the most important stage of creation. Believe that you have received all those blessings you prayed for or sought.

There are people who constantly put God on trial through their blame, ingratitude, and discontentment. I talk of Muhammad Ali's generation, which did not have self-belief to become great, but worse, there were people who lived and died without really living. They lived as victims of others or external conditions. They felt powerless and worthless, ashamed of themselves. Well, each spent their life as they chose. What if Ali had lived as powerless victim, regretting his life and blaming others and giving up on his dreams? We would not have had Ali.

Muhammad Ali never said he would be the world's greatest, or he would be the world's greatest after beating so and so. He said, "I am the world's greatest." *Will be* or *would be* would have confirmed his lack and neediness. He knew that he already was the world's greatest, and I believe no greater boxer came before or after him. He had supreme faith in the infinite intelligence that knew no impossible. Those who believed in lack or didn't have faith in infinite intelligence withheld those resources from themselves; they denied themselves and the world their talents and skills or ideas or inventions. The truth of infinite intelligence is too hard for them to understand because they believe in illusions and egoistic thoughts of lack and limitation and impossibility. It is as easy to have these infinite resources, as it is easy not to have them.

Those resources do not come from outside, but it is just unlocking those infinite resources within you. It is opening the tap to allow the flow out of the infinite intelligence and abundance within. It is recognizing or accepting its presence within. It is a conscious and right-minded recognition. The ego suppresses or veils this recognition of the unlimited intelligence, resources, power, wealth, talent, skills, ideas, and other blessings within you.

To the level you recognize and accept this infinite abundance within you is equally proportion the level of your abundance, success, wealth, and other blessings in your external life. You consciously or unconsciously determine the level of success, wealth, abundance, or other blessings you have in your life (it is not wanting to have, which means confirmation of their lack, and it is not recognizing what you had, as this is created by past illusions of lack, scarcity, limitation, or poverty). Both are equally life-wasting illusions and egoistic.

The ego sometimes, since the past is gone, with evidence or experience, cleverly attaches its worth to anticipation of a better, happy, or abundant future. Therefore, again, the past already wasted, the ego now wastes your present time or the now through anticipation, seeking, or looking forward to it. This is based on the illusion that you do not have or lack these resources like talent, skills, wealth, health, peace, or other blessings now. Therefore, you look forward to those blessings in the future. Here you get a feeling of lack, in search of purpose because you are discontented now. Remember, the ego wasted your past with those same feelings of lack but here promises to give you those blessings in the future. But for most people, their past illusions or identities or thoughts of lack or scarcity create their present life or their future. So, they expect almost no change or believe the presence of abundance within. They have lived most or all their past lives in their self-limiting identity created by the ego. They cannot easily accept the new reality or truth of infinite abundance within. They constantly fall back to those old self-limiting identities or illusions of lack, such that they continue living a life of scarcity even after learning of the new truth. Learning the new truth or wisdom is not enough. You have to live according to the new wisdom daily and by consciously ignoring the old illusion as a wandering of the mind.

The best way to live according to this eternal truth is to constantly practice stillness and remember or reflect on your new wisdom or enlightenment. Significantly reduce or eliminate the distractions, such as unnecessary chats, TV, social media, and other activities that are stealing away and distracting you from stillness, conscious thoughts and living, meditation, or enlightenment. You cannot cling to your old habits or schedules or lifestyle and yet want to live in a new reality of abundance and wisdom. For most, they continue living in lack, poverty, or scarcity, not because they reject or have not read about enlightened life but because they find it hard to detach themselves from their old realities or identities created by the illusion of lack. Even if they live in scarcity, lack, pain, and other illusions, they see the ego and their past illusions as too real to forget or detach from. They think it is too hard to get out of this image of self-limits. The past illusions look too real; they believe this is their fate, destiny, and that good things, infinite intelligence, resources, and abundance or success or great wealth belong to others. They look at themselves as undeserving. They think, *How can I write a great book when in the past I found it difficult to write even a page?* Or they didn't have good writing skills or language proficiency, or they were told that that were not good enough, or they got a bad grade in school because they used to live in the illusions of scarcity, lack, and an identity of "I am not good enough." Their past failures, scarcity, lack, and the opinions in form of verbal expressions and grades in school were all created by their illusions of a negative past self-image, such as lacking intelligence, skills, talents, and other thoughts of scarcity. This illusion gave them those results, realities, opinions, self-images, identities, and other misfortunes and bad experiences. Here we see that illusions of a negative self-image and beliefs and identities led them to have bad past, failures, or results, which were real and can be seen and evidenced externally. What is not real are the illusions of a negative self-image, scarcity, and self-limit, but not the results or outcomes created by them. Wrong-mindedness, ignorance, unconsciousness, and illusions produced those results or realities.

You reap what you sow. As expected, illusions produce disappointment, failure, and discontentment. What changed is those illusions are now replaced by wisdom or knowledge of the truth about infinite resources, and abundance within. In the past, your illusion of lacking them brought you lack, failure, pain, and misery. Now the knowledge of the truth or thoughts of right-mindedness and faith will bring you abundance, success, happiness, and other blessings. In the past, you sowed failure, scarcity, pain, or lack, and you reaped their fruit (products). Now you sow abundance, success, and other blessings, and you will reap their fruits (products). When I say your reality or past is not real, I mean what created those realities—your illusions and wrong-mindedness—are not real.

Not Real or Truth Creates Reality/Real Results

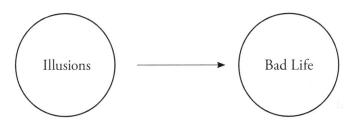

Real Reality / Real Results

Creates

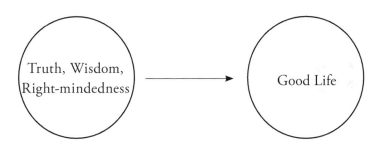

You see both results are real (feedback is your reality or the kind of life you will have). So, what makes it difficult for people to detach from the past is they focus on the past results rather than what caused them. The past results gave them their identities, and for sure they have lived through those experiences or results that are tangible and have empirical evidence. They were of course real and can be easily remembered, and you can even have several eyewitnesses who can confirm and collaborate those results or your experiences. These witnesses and you, have created opinions of who you are, based on those results or experiences. This is because you focused on why squeezing an orange produced orange juice or why planting an orange seed resulted in an orange tree. Of course, the results were real, as the juice is real and the process of growth is real.

The wisdom, the truth, and the enlightenment or the new reality or change here is the seed, and that should be your focus. What kind of seed did you plant? The results are obvious and expected. Here, we look at your egoistic thoughts and the illusion of lack and failure and the negative self-image that gave you those results or final products. No surprise, the orange seed gave you the orange plant. As well, your new knowledge of the truth or enlightenment about the presence of infinite intelligence within you, will result in success, abundance, wealth, happiness, and other blessings.

Do not focus on those past identities or the results created by your illusions or egoistic thoughts. Do not even focus on how, why, and what created those illusions. Instead, focus on the new seed of thoughts or identities created by knowledge of the truth, wisdom, or enlightenment or right-mindedness now. The results are guaranteed, as in the past where illusion or wrong-mindedness and egoistic thoughts of scarcity, failure, and lack gave you bad life. Your new seed of enlightenment and right-mindedness will give you a good life of success, abundance, good health, happiness, intelligence, and other blessings. You will reap what you sow.

If you filled in the wrong address on your GPS, when you got there and realized it was the wrong house, you would not just walk into the house and stay there. You would call and ask your hosts for the right address and put in the right address and drive over to their house. The wrong address is the same as wrong-mindedness or illusions that led you to your destiny (destination) of failures, scarcity, and other problems. So, why do you insist on staying in the wrong house or destination? Why do you accept the wrong house (destiny) as your true destination (destiny)? Learn or ask for the right address (right-mindedness or enlightenment) and drive to your right destination (destiny) of success, abundance, peace, and good health.

Stop dwelling on the wrong address. Get the new address and start driving (living) to the right destiny or life.

Independence

True independence means true life. You should not depend on people, including friends, family members, bosses, or leaders. You should not depend on institutions like schools, hospitals, churches, companies, or governments. You should not depend on masters, spiritual leaders, meditations, books, or seminars. You should not depend on social media or TV. You should not depend on food, drinks, drugs, or smoking. You should depend on nothing and no one but yourself. You have the infinite intelligence within you, which has everything in this world in abundance. When you abandon your dependence on outside forces and focus on the infinite intelligence and abundance within, then miracles start happening. You will realize that you already have everything you needed in this world. You are infinitely abundant and a genius. You have all the answers within. The answer to your life lies within you.

Creation and Underused Power of Mind

You are creating your future, destiny, and reality all the time, even during those times you thought you were bored or had no particular thoughts in mind. To be bored or have idle thoughts is a sign that you are greatly underusing the power of your mental thoughts and the power of your creations and the infinite intelligence within. It also means you are wasting away the most precious moment of your life, which is the now. These idle thoughts and boredom are due to your ignorance of the power of the infinite intelligence within you, it is a failure to use your mental power and imagination, which is one of the greatest and infinite resources we possess. Imagine, each second can be used to imagine and create a great life for yourself and others, just through your mental power. Any of those seconds can change the world or the way we live. How many seconds do you have to imagine and create? Think how you have been unconsciously wasting your life and potential through boredom and idle thoughts. Value your time. Value those seconds to empower yourself and the people around you.

It is the underused or wasted mind that is poor and creates all the poor conditions for you. These minds are wasted by low energies or negative emotions and illusions such as fear, scarcity, confusion, lack, discontentment, anxiety, low self-esteem, and so on. All these are diseases of the mind that bring poverty and suffering to your life.

Creation, Wastage, and Universal Law

You cannot create infinite intelligence, power, faith, or abundance. You can only create consciously the right environment or right-mindedness for the universal mind to manifest itself in your life. Remove the veil for infinite intelligence, power, faith, and abundance to flow out, manifest, and create a good life for you and others.

You experience failure and frustration because of your attempt to create what is not creatable or in your capacity to create. When you try to create infinite intelligence, faith, power, and abundance, you soon realize that your time and energy are too limited, and the goals are too far out of your reach. You can clench your teeth, gather your energy, and psyche up yourself, but it will be all in vain. You can create your conscious thoughts, beliefs, and perspective but not eternal truths, divine imagination, and intuitions.
The knowledge of what you can create and should create will save you a lot of time and energy. Things will happen for you effortlessly and naturally, because you are following the universal laws or laws of nature. Therefore, there is zero possibility of failure and frustration. You will also enjoy and appreciate every single moment of your life (the present moment) because nature or the universal laws do not depend on or need your sacrifice of the present moment or failure to achieve success or greatness. Nature or universal law will not lead you to wastage of your time, energy, peace, or integrity in the

present moment for a better future. For nature and universal law, each moment is a success and precious.

Celebration Instead of Thanks

Gratitude is only half a celebration of the good things in your life. It is better to choose words to celebrate and appreciate life other than just saying thank you. When you say thank you, whenever you are by yourself to show gratitude for a good life, that is communication of your inner thoughts and feelings, which are generally good. Of course, "thank you" is better than saying nothing at all. The best practice is coming up with your own words that expresses your appreciation. For example, using words like amazing, wonderful, supreme, I love it, and so on. There are so many other words you can use to expresses your joy, contentment, or acceptance.

1. What Is Gratitude?

Gratitude is finding victory in every situation. It is transmuting everything into victory and into good. It is telling others and yourself that you just won, you are winning, and you will be winning. It is having the victorious attitude and actions. Gratitude is not just saying thank you at night after a long day of whining and negative thoughts.

The new perspective on gratitude and meditation will make you feel more powerful. This is because you take back the power and forces that you have given out to external things. This is a process of reintegration that makes your spiritual world supremely solid. The expending of those forces and power to external things is disintegration of spiritual wholeness. In disintegration, you give away your power, confidence, integrity, and control to outside forces. Reintegration is taking all these things back and becoming whole again spiritually. It is reclaiming your kingdom.

Life Is about Celebrating Small Moments

Life is a about celebrating the small moments daily rather than waiting to celebrate the bigger victories later. Practice this and you will live a happy life. When you learn to celebrate the small victories and accomplishments, you will learn to recognize and celebrate the bigger victories.

Unlike in sports, the ordinary person does not celebrate the small daily victories and instead focuses on the small daily inconveniences and perceived failures. If you only celebrate the daily seemingly small victories, then it won't be long before the big victories come along. If you do not know how to celebrate the small victories, then you will not know how to celebrate the big ones, and you may even fail to notice or appreciate those victories.

A goal scorer in a soccer game will celebrate the goal even though they do not know if they will win the game in the end. The important thing here is not the end result but the celebration of the goal, which in turn gives you the excitement and energy to win the game in the end. Do not wait for that big achievement so that you can celebrate life; it will probably never come if you do not start celebrating the small victories now.

The lack of celebrating these small achievements will lead you into believing that you are getting nowhere and a feeling of stagnation. This is largely because you overlooked and failed to celebrate the small victories that would have led to the bigger ones eventually, as a result of getting energized and motivated by the smaller victories.

Look for something to celebrate each day and each hour, and you will find there are so many of them. The excitement and energy you receive from these small victories will lead you to greater and unimaginable victories. Write them down in your diary daily. Make a habit of celebrating them as they happen.

Victim Identity

7

Drop of Blood

In the animal kingdom, if a predator sees an injured animal,
The injured will be singled out and becomes an easy kill and meal.
That instinct is within us still.
If people find out your weakness and that you're ill,
They will go after you just like an easy meal.
You will be singled out, humiliated, and attacked.
Even the weakest and the most fearful gain strength
When they find someone weaker than they are.
They will, by instinct, adopt this nature's game,
Unless they are well-disciplined and enlightened to tame.
This animal instinct within all of us is the same.
Some people can take advantage and make your life hell.
Sometimes even the people who treat everyone else well.
But your victim identity will influence them to act ill
Because they see you as defenseless and easy to attack
And can get away with anything without fearing a payback.
Your weakness will bring out the animal nature in them.
You become an easy target for anyone to take.
You are so tempting to be humiliated and badly treated.
Please do not die like that.
Do not show your injury or weakness to people.

Cover up and be brave and accept no debacle,
As injuries and defeats will not last for long.
We are all born fearless and supremely strong.
The weakness and sense of injury is misguided knowledge,
Adopted as a result of challenges and wrong self-image.
Do not tempt others to come and attack you.
Do not bring out the bad nature in others by revealing your weakness.
Don't be a bad influence on others and bring out their meanness.
Do not tell people how life or others have treated you bad
Because you will be inviting them to treat you the same.
Talk of your strength, victories, and of the good in your life,
And everyone and everything will be good to you likewise.
Cover your injuries and perceived weaknesses.
Otherwise it will take away your joy and happiness,
Because exposing your weakness or injuries will be inviting
Spiritual death and greater suffering,
The moment you give away a victim statement,
Explaining your suffering and defeats,
Thus giving away your power to the people you confess.
Never ever complain about anything or anyone else,
Even to yourself, and that is where the journey should start

The Weak Target

During hunting, lions and other predators go after the wounded or the weak. Human beings use the same instinct; when you show weakness, anybody and everybody will come after you. Never ever show weakness, or you become a target. I was watching an Arsenal versus Everton game. The goal keeper (Ospina) got injured and was limping in the game. The Everton players acted like a feeding frenzy to take advantage of the injury to score goals. It's amazing how you can attract an attack if people notice your weakness. If Ospina pretended to be well and walked straight, it would not have caused this frenzy. Never cause a feeding frenzy by exposing your weaknesses.

A friend you tell your problem to will be your next problem unless they are very close and loyal to you. When you get a little close to someone and tell them your problem, they will turn around and use that information and those victim statements against you. Now you will have to live in fear of them telling people about your problems and secrets. They will look at you as a weak person who can be taken advantage of, and they will try to do the same thing to you or use your story to attack you next time. They will lose respect for you.

Don't tell everyone your perceived weaknesses, because if you look deep within, you will realize how strong you are, and your problems will look really insignificant. You have infinite intelligence and infinite strength to rely on within you. You will be amazed at the heights you will reach and how fast your problems will go away.

Tell your friends your strength, and you will be stronger, and they will strengthen you, and they will grow stronger because of you. When you tell your friends your problems and weaknesses, you bring them down with your low energies. You will lose your friendship with them. You will be a source of negative and toxic energy to your friends and surroundings. Open your eyes and start spreading strength, power, joy, happiness, peace, courage, abundance, and health. They are waiting for your blessings; share them with them. Make your friends better people by making them stronger through channeling a positive energy. You have been a source of pain and weakness; now be a source of strength and happiness.

The habit of seeking sympathy from others and giving sympathy to others is dangerous and life wasting. It is life wasting because, to seek sympathy, you think of yourself as a victim of circumstances or people. These thoughts and behaviors sack the life energy out of you and become self-fulfilling.

Different Mentality of Solving Problems

When it comes to solving problems, the mental attitude of a victim and a victor are different.

The victim is thinking of how things are happening to them and how their hand is forced to react in a certain way, and on their minds are what stories to tell of how they were targeted by a situation or a person.

On the other hand, the victor thinks of how they are in control of a situation and acts according to their principles and plans but does not think of themselves as being forced to react. The victor's mental story is that of winning and does not allow the situation to determine their feelings or reactions. They act based on their principles and philosophies of life.

Reclaiming Your Kingdom and Power

As I experienced in my life, just like many before me, I came back to myself and reclaimed my kingdom. This rigorous spiritual journey endows you with amazing power over yourself as stated at the beginning of this book. All the searching brings you back to where you began. You start seeing yourself and other things with a different perspective. You start recognizing the immense power, intelligence, courage, and wealth that lies within you.

Many people are living with illusions of who they are, and they die never realizing their power and true potential. The process itself is painful until you regain your kingdom and truly know who you are. Sometimes you are even brought to this process because of unimaginable pain or failure you went through in life.

Most people don't realize themselves because they have not reached that threshold of failure or pain. Many will go through life with a decent level of success and settle with a family and a secure job. This decent or average success in life will not necessitate a deep soul search. I understand if some people prefer not to go through the pain and instead choose an average and uneventful, conventional life. I would have chosen the same kind of life while I was still going through the process, but now after reclaiming my kingdom, I would accept the same pain and process to get to this point. I would do it all over again and choose the same life to get this wisdom and enlightenment.

The process is painful because you realize what a fool you were in blaming other people for all the things you did to yourself and all that life-wasting energy you have been harboring. You are a very lucky person if you successfully go through this process before your death. This is the most important education. All the formal education you received in school was to teach you how to become someone's employee. This education will teach you how to become a master of your life and destiny.

Faith and wisdom to reclaim your kingdom

In the past, if you were knocking on others' doors and begging for a bowl of rice or worthless coins or seeking your treasures outside e.g. in career/professional jobs fulfilment, wife, wealth, spiritual fulfilment or others' favourable opinions etc. Reclaim your kingdom and stop the begging. Discover your limitless treasures within, this treasure is your faith guided by right-mindedness/wisdom/enlightenment/consciousness. This infinite treasure is not external wealth, talent, writing skills, courage, confidence, happiness peace of mind, good health etc. All these are the manifestation of the infinite intelligence/infinite power within (God). So, God (infinite intelligence within) are the sources of all those blessings manifested in your life. The infinite treasure itself is faith guided by wisdom, while infinite scarcity or suffering is faith guide by ignorance (unconscious faith). Here the common denominator is faith, which is equally powerful in both cases. Faith with wisdom makes you the king of your great empire, while faith with ignorance makes you a beggar. The difference between a king and a beggar is wisdom/enlightenment/right-mindedness, consciousness. You see this evidence in your every day life, both are miracles. Unconscious/ignorant faith creates a life of scarcity, poverty, pain, suffering, fear, worry, anxiety, bad health, discontent, unhappiness, doubt, confusion, uncertainty, failure, victim hood, weakness, dependence, begging, anger, ingratitude, negative self-image, stress, lack of love for self and others, a feeling of worthlessness and undeserving of good things in life, feeling unlucky and unfortunate, mental enslavement and restlessness etc. (its hell).

On the other hand, conscious/enlightened faith (faith with wisdom/right-mindedness) creates a life of infinite abundance, intelligence, wealth, happiness, peace of mind, independence, power, certainty, confidence, good health, contentment, calm/serenity, astronomical success, loving yourself and others, a great sense of self-worth and positive self-image, a feeling of deserving all the good thing in life, feeling of luck/fortune and mental freedom etc. (it's is heaven). It is the only heaven, these are the treasures in your kingdom/empire. Knowing about it is not enough you have to believe it/have faith and accept it as your only true treasure and reality. It is knowing and accepting that all your external manifestations/ blessings/success depends on only what you create in your invisible world. So, you have power over what you want to create and manifest in your life, it does not depend on your circumstances/conditions, other people, institutions, background, country, marital status, past, your way of life, luck, network, connection, marketing, CV, education level, others opinions/acceptance, hard work, experience or spiritual purity. Accept and live by this truth and create whatever kind of life you want.

You don't accept this truth because you want to create a good life/success for yourself, but because it is the truth, it is the universal law. In the past, all your problems, sufferings, lack, begging etc. were because; you were ignorant (didn't know the truth) or you knew the truth but ignored or postponed its acceptance (ego's work), or because you doubted the truth. You shall know the truth and the truth shall set you free now! All the infinite blessings and astronomical success are all your eternal rights that you deserve as much as anyone else in this world. They don't depend on anything or anyone, they don't depend on favors/goodness of people, institutions, your personal life history, past or current situations/circumstances, not on others opinions/acceptance/beliefs etc. This is total supreme independence, freedom and power. You create your own conditions/circumstances. Thinking or believing that your life or success/ blessings depend on anything or anyone, means you are giving away your power, independence and freedom to those things or people, it means you abandoned/gave away/left your palace and empire to beg for a bowl of rice or worthless coins. Why do you choose to become a beggar? Why do you remove your kings rob to put on servant dress/uniform? Why do you give away your infinite treasures, wealth, blessings, power, independence and freedom to beg from others? In the past, I have abandoned my empire and lived a life of a slave and a beggar, there is nothing good about it. when I could beg no more, fail no more, break universal laws no more and become a slave no more, because I hit rock bottom, I came back to my kingdom/empire/palace and treasures, I am blessed and lucky for getting the chance to comeback. Independence/power/freedom/infinite treasures and abundance are so sweet. I will never give them away, no to anyone or anything. This truth is the true source of confidence, assurance/certainty, peace of mind and complete faith. Confidence and certainty comes out of this truth. Thus, this truth is the foundation of all greatness in this world. This truth will immediately change how you think and act. It will become the foundation and source of all your actions and thoughts, circumstances and conditions. Although sometimes things seem to you as happenings by chance or as a result of external influence or action, but the truth is, they are not happening by chance or as a result of other people or external influence. They are exactly happening according to your beliefs/invisible creation i.e. according to this truth/your acceptance/wisdom and faith. You may not connect the dots looking forward, but once you witness its manifestation, you will be able to connect them looking backward.

So, consciously observe and understand that everything happens solely to bring about the manifestation of this truth in your life. Sometimes, you may feel or think that what you are experiencing or experienced are the opposite of what you expect or thought of fulfilling this truth but looking back you will find that was or is exactly needed to fulfill or manifest this truth. Everything happens for the good of this truth. So, don't be surprised, worried, confused or doubt because of some events, thoughts, actions or circumstances that you think are against the fulfillment of this truth. The universe has its way of manifesting your faith/beliefs/dwelling thoughts/invisible creations.

So, all happens, happened and will happen towards the fulfillment of this truth/your invisible creation/your dwelling thoughts/your beliefs. These happenings include; yours' or others' thoughts and actions, external events and circumstances, your past and present and future, (everything you saw, you see or you may see as good or bad). But for the universe (universal law), they are all good, they are perfectly working, worked or will work to fulfill/manifest your invisible creations/faith/beliefs/dwelling thoughts. So, accept everything as blessings, as building blocks that are needed for manifestations of your invisible creations/faith/beliefs/dwelling thoughts, even those moments of doubts that come s a result of wondering away of the mind. So, live according to your faith/invisible creation and never be surprised, disappointed, saddened, angered or doubt what happens on this path (the path of invisible creation.

Stop focusing on your past performances

You find many artists, writers, sport stars etc. who were held back by their past performances. They focus on their past great performances and fear that they could not reproduce or surpass that performance again, this doubts and thoughts of looking back will eventually limit their performances and set a boundary for them. This is also true in all other aspects of life. See yesterday's thoughts and actions as dead. Everyday die to the past or yesterday. Arm yourself with the power of the present moment each new day. Dying to the past and yesterday, will make you truly live today.

Most people live in fear, confusion and worry because they believe what they truly possess are, their; status, jobs/careers, school certificates, fame, wealth (e.g. house, cars, money, investments, insurance policy, other peoples' opinion and approval, marital/ spousal support, financial security, retirement plans and security, etc. All the above are things that are not truly yours or are in your control. They don't really/truly belong to you. Also, the past and the future do not belong to you, so stop thinking or worrying about them and stop making references to the past to determine your happiness, success, performance, creativity, writings, decisions, actions, reactions/responses, perception, self-image, courage, confidence, wisdom, health, fearlessness, contentment, wealth, faith, beliefs etc. The past has no power to determine/influence your today. Likewise, the future should not determine/influence your today, in terms of all those things mentioned above. The past or the future should not determine what you create now or today in your invisible world. The past will create self-limitations thoughts, regrets, guilt etc. which will perpetuate your past negative self image, ignorance, unconscious and negative dwelling thoughts/ illusions mistakes and failures. While worrying about the future will result in anxiety, fear, perturbations, confusions, uncertainty, doubt, self-limiting thoughts and actions in order to prepare for anticipated future outcomes. Therefore, you should live today unconditionally, without reference to the past (yesterday) or in anticipation of tomorrow (the future). And only then, will today (the power of NOW) reveal its infinite power, intelligence, genius, happiness, contentment and other gifts.

You will experience the miracle of living in the present moment, it will give you automatic fearlessness/courage, peace of mind and contentment/satisfaction. It is true independence, creativity and abundance will flow out of you non-stop.

Not fearing does not mean, you stop creating in your invisible world or having positive mental dwelling. But it means, living in faith, you accept those things you want to manifest in your life (your prayers/mental dwellings) as received. So, someone who has already received, why should he be afraid or doubt if he will receive? You can only deny or withhold from yourself by those thoughts of doubts, worry and fear. And if you think, your receiving (manifestation) or visible reality outcomes depended on other people (their opinion, approval or acceptance), then you are denying/withholding from yourself the manifestation of those blessings/receiving those blessings. Since those thoughts of dependence will result in lack of faith through doubts, fear and anxiety. You cannot say, "God (infinite intelligence within) will bless me (make me receive), but this blessing (receiving) depends on others opinion, approval and acceptance". If you believe God (infinite intelligence within) is infinitely powerful, then you have to realize and accept that, this power depends on no one and nothing, have faith in infinite intelligence and live in faith all your life. As within, so without. Your invisible creation will soon be your visible/manifested reality. So, fearing nothing and no one, depending on nothing and no one, will make you truly independent and free. Since it will make you realize, you have God (infinite intelligence) within you, that makes you infinitely powerful to create your present conditions/circumstances, your future/destiny/fate etc. You need no fear or dependence in your invisible creation/dwelling thoughts, in order to manifest whatever level of success, happiness etc. in your life. Since when did fear and dependence support you in creating a good future/success or present conditions for you? How can making yourself sick brings health?

The Power of Your Choices and Consequences

When you throw an orange in the air, there is only one possible outcome: the orange will come back to hit the ground because of earth's gravity. In life, when you choose an action, the outcomes are beyond your control; the laws of nature, just like gravity, will determine the outcome. Do not ever worry about the outcome of your work. Just focus on your actions, and the results are guaranteed by the same universal law. Again, the power to choose is in your hands but not the consequences.

Choose good health, happiness, peace, courage, abundance, blessing, joy, intelligence, calmness, love, gratitude, strength, wealth, power, and contentment.

You also have the power to choose your response to an event or others' actions. Each choice you make has a consequence that will decide how you feel inside and what you can achieve externally and your health. Your life will be a consequence of those choices you make.

Don't let the ego make you believe that you are forced to make a certain choice as a result of other people's actions. Do not give that power to anyone or any circumstance. Do not choose your career because that is what the economy needs. The economy is created by you and for you; you are not created for the economy. You are not a piece of a puzzle that is created to complete the economic juggernaut. You are the creator of the puzzle. You are not a robot being designed to serve the system; instead, the system should serve you.

You should not let the opinion of others decide what career you choose. You should not be fooled by the frivolous idea of status or to look a part. Do not become a prisoner of expectations. Do not be pressured by others' opinions about what you should become or should not become when making career choices. Do not let others make you abandon your intuition or true calling.

Living Fully in This World

At the beginning of my spiritual journey, I used to think that the spiritual life was too good and soft to live in this world. I was sometimes too nice and thought it was impossible to live in this world as an enlightened person. Now I laugh at those ideas. It was the egoistic mind creating a sense of separation and incompatibility with current time and circumstances of my life.

I was born in a perfect world, at the perfect time, and in the perfect place and had perfect life experiences that brought me to this perfect moment. What happened in the past was the egoistic mind fighting to stay longer and hence creating this feeling of mismatch between the spiritual and the visible or conventional world. It was the last of the ego's fight to hold on to false identity, a misfit and alienation. Now it is all gone with a simple observation of the wandering mind and ignoring the silly ideas. Even those feelings were an important part of the journey. You will come to learn that nothing you went through is in vain if you find a way of making it useful.

End of Illusions

The end of the egoistic mind will be the beginning of a new and more beautiful world for you. It will be the dawning of a new era marked by truly living and enjoying the present moment. It's when you will see beauty in everything and everyone. It's when you become one with life. It is the realization that you are part of the infinite universe that contains everything you see and you don't see, everything you hated and loved, every good and bad emotion, every failure and success. It is like a jar filled with every type of grain in the world, and you are one of the grains, and you stop asking why all the other grains do not look like you.

Spiritual Orgasm

For me, it is that moment when you experience and see the world in a completely different light—in purity, without any thought, calculations, judgment, or references. People may call it intuition, hunches, or revelation, but I call it spiritual orgasm. The moment is sweet, so pure and personal. It comes from time to time, and I wish it to stay forever, but then I realize I should be grateful for the period it comes rather than feel sorry that it ended. Who wants to have an orgasm the whole day? It would lose its sweetness and become tiresome. After getting that moment of spiritual orgasm, I am left with an intellectual analysis and explanation of what I just experienced or felt.

8

Power of Belief and Faith

The Knife (Power) in Your Hands

The power to create a good life for our ourselves and others is our birthright. This power comes from the infinite intelligence within. Let's think of this power as a knife in our hands. All of us already have the knife (power) in our hand from birth. All that is needed is to learn how to cook good food (good life) for ourselves and others using this knife (power). As your birthright, there are no preconditions necessary for you to get this power. You need not be a good person, enlightened, wise, right-minded, conscious, strong, or learned to get this knife (power), but you need all of those to cook good food and make a good life using this knife (power). The people who cooked bad food (had a bad life) or used the knife to hurt themselves or others (a bad life for themselves and others) did not have the right-mindedness, salvation, wisdom, truth, enlightenment, and so on. The bad food (bad life) is a result of their ignorance or lack of proper skills to use their knife (power). In this group, we also have people who are unaware that they were born with a knife (power) in their hands. Therefore, they cannot cook for themselves and their families; hence they sleep hungry, and they are poor and beg others for leftovers. Their ignorance produces lack and scarcity. They don't have the knife only because they don't know they were born with it. Both of these groups live in illusion, suffering, and doubt. The doubt of whether you have this knife or power in your hand also makes you suffer. Wisdom, truth, right-mindedness, consciousness, and enlightenment remove these doubts from your mind.

How big is that power? It is infinite. You see it doing miracles, healing the sick, and in people who changed their lives from rags to riches. You see this power in the works of Albert Einstein, Steve Jobs, Isaac Newton, Michelangelo, Henry Ford, the Wright brothers, and all other inventors, billionaires, poets, philosophers, writers, musicians, sages, and spiritual leaders and in many other people from all walks of life. All the amazing creations and inventions I see every day that I used to think were impossible for me to invent or understand or use properly.

On the other hand, you also see the work of this infinite power destroying lives, creating bad lives for others, in the works of Adolf Hitler, Mussolini, Stalin, and in extreme poverty, suffering, pain, sickness, failure, and misery. Just like the knowledge of using the knife (power) to cook good food (create a good life) or cook bad food (a bad life for you and others), the outcome depends on your skills and choices.

I came to learn that all I was doing in the past few years was learning how to use my knife (power) to cook good food for myself and others. I was not seeking or searching or begging or praying to get the knife (power); we all already have it. Now that you know you have the knife (power) in your hands, what kind of food do you want to cook for yourself and others (what kind of life do want to have)?

The knife (power) is infinitely powerful but cannot teach you how to cook, and it does not come with instructions and does not come with automation to cook for you by itself. How fast is the knife (power) to cook? It is infinitely fast and infinitely powerful. But the speed of the cooking depends on your skills of using the knife (power). You can go extremely slow or fast. The speed comes with your level of enlightenment, right-mindedness, consciousness, and knowledge of the universal laws. All this means the same thing—how well you can use your knife to cook good food (good life).

You have to give back this knife (power) at the end of your life (death takes it away). The length of time you keep this knife (power) depends on your skills, which in turn determines your health. You need good health and right-mindedness to cook good food in the shortest time possible. Speed and good health are important factors; the sooner, the better. Bad health and old age reduce your speed and skills but do not take away the knife (power) from your hands.

You cannot give your knife (power) to another person. We were all given the same knife (power), but you can teach others how they can use their knife (power) skillfully to cook good food (have a good life for themselves and others). You have to have good cooking skills to cook good food.

The fact that you have the knife (power) in your hand does not mean you will cook good food (have a good life). Everybody has a knife (power) in their hands, but not everybody will cook good food (have a good life).

The Relationship between Your Dhabbinn and the Knife (Power)

Holding on to your dhabbinn means holding on to your skills, integrity, peace, and so on in order to cook the best food. So, love, contentment, enlightenment, being one with life, and so on are all the necessary skills to become a good cook or have a good life.

When you are stressed, perturbed, hateful, and full of guilt, fear, and regrets and other low energies, you will not be able to cook good food, and you will not enjoy the cooking and eating. You will just waste your life or time in the kitchen. It means you wasted your short time in the kitchen (on this earth) on low energies and pain, hating, and complaining, not paying attention to your cooking, which resulted in bad food (a bad life), and you ended up not enjoying your dinner. You just wasted everything. Finally, you will go to bed (death) with all this heaviness, filled with low energies. Why? Yet not everybody is lucky like you to see their bed (old age). Some lives were taken by others' knives or their own. Some others could not finish the cooking because of bad health or other factors, and others left before even knowing how to hold their knife (power) and did not get any time in the kitchen or had no time at all (died young).

Others wasted their lives or time in the kitchen, just standing there with their knives in their hands, confused, doubting themselves, afraid to cook and analyzing everything in their lives. There is just too much on their minds. They cannot cook, and before they know it, their time in the kitchen is up. They beg and eat others' leftovers. They never had any proper dinner or good food (a good life). They never cooked, or some started but stopped the cooking at some point (they never or barely tried to do something in their lives). They never complete anything in their life. They never or barely used their knives.

Use your knife (power) wisely, to cook good food (a good life) for yourself and others.

Faith

We are all born with faith. Nobody on this earth is without faith (to label or call people as faithless is wrong and inaccurate). We are all faithful or have faith. There is no strong or weak faith. There is no powerful or powerless faith (all faith is infinitely powerful). We all have infinite faith that can bring fortune or misfortune to our lives based on our perspective, wisdom, or beliefs. The only difference is what kind of faith you have, the wrong faith (through wrong-mindedness) that is creating a bad life for you and others or the right faith (through right-mindedness) that is creating a good life for you and others. The wrong faith is the negative perspective or illusion you have about yourself and the world. In this case, you may see yourself as a failure, weak, miserable, poor, sick, fearful, anxious, unlucky, unfulfilled, incomplete, discontent, unhappy, unworthy, undesirable, unintelligent, unattractive, unskillful, untalented, timid, sinful, unsettled, confused, unfriendly, unprincipled, ungodly, addict, self-doubting, undeserving, unlovable, awkward, selfish, unfriendly, ungrateful, lonely, slow, powerless, lazy, dependent, a loser, a victim, and many other negative self-images and perspectives. These negative thoughts and beliefs form your infinitely powerful faith that ultimately creates your reality accordingly. On the other hand, the right faith is based on positive perspective and truths about yourself and the world. In this case, you may see yourself as powerful, intelligent, talented, skillful, important, peaceful, happy, rich, friendly, generous, confident, courageous, deserving, worthy, disciplined, hardworking, lucky, attractive, healthy, contented, grateful, strong, principled, winner, lovable, calm, self-controlled, independent, accurate, fast, self-assured, and many other positive self-images and perspectives. Equally, your faith in these thoughts and beliefs creates your reality.

Also, your belief of having no faith is also a wrong faith. The question is not whether you have faith or not; it is whether you have the right or the wrong faith. You cannot strengthen your faith; it is already strong. You cannot seek or search for faith; it is already within you. You cannot compare the strength of your faith with others; they are all equally strong. Nobody can give you faith or take it away from you, and you cannot train to be faithful. You are already faithful. But you can learn to be conscious, enlightened, and wise to gain right-mindedness in order to use your faith to create a good life for you and others.

Being one with God or the infinite intelligence is when your conscious and subconscious mind are in harmony to create a good life for you and others. Here, your subconscious mind is creating what you have thought and planned consciously. It means you are right-minded, so you are aware of the power of your thoughts that impresses and write the orders of what you want to create, and the subconscious mind creates or follows those orders. It means you are not surprised and can never be disappointed by the outcome or creations of your subconscious mind. You understand what you typed is what you will print or get from the printer. No other outcomes are possible here. You understand how realities, dreams, or your current future is created. It is not a guess, and it not by chance or by luck or as a result of external conditions or circumstances.

The separation, confusion, ignorance, poverty, disappointments, and disharmony happen when you don't understand the universal laws. It is when you unconsciously think or dwell on thoughts of failure, poverty, scarcity, lack, fear, doubt, bad future, or other unpleasant things, and you get surprised or disappointed when those things become a reality in your life. You think of A and expect B to happen, or you type A and expect to see B on the printout. There is certainty, assurance, and guarantee in success but not in failure. That is why you see successful people are self-assured, confident, and certain, because they know there is no chance, luck, or uncertainty in their lives. They have complete faith that what you sow is what you harvest. These people do not expect surprises because of this simple rule. What you typed on the screen of your subconscious mind is what you will get in your life. Doubt is misunderstanding or ignorance of this law but not an emotion or a feeling; it is intellectual. Whatever your goals are, small or big, bad or good, supreme or basic, they are guaranteed to come true or be achieved or realized based on the message you typed on the screen of your subconscious mind.

You don't create the universal laws. You just understand and follow them (life's current). If you don't follow them, you will live in misery, pain, failure, uncertainty, fear, and doubt. Just like if you ignore a country's secular laws, you will end up in jail or face other types of punishment. Your ignorance will not offer you any defense against the application and execution of these laws, just as with the laws of nature. These universal laws were here before you were born and will be here eternally. You cannot break or destroy the universal laws; you can only break yourself against them. Take care of the messaging or what you want to type because it is what you will get on the printer soon (in the form of your realities and life's conditions).

The Relationship between Dwelling Thoughts or Faith and Your Realities

The subconscious mind receives orders and instructions from the conscious mind, but do these orders have to be repeated for the subconscious mind to create those realities? Is the reaffirmation or repetition done to strengthen your faith or make a clear imprint on the subconscious mind? The reaffirmations or repetitions are to convince your conscious mind to accept your new aspirations or goals and become your dwelling thought. Faith is already infinitely powerful and strong, but the strength of your dwelling thought varies. It can be doubtful, nonexistent, or very strong (forms your faith). The repetition or reaffirmation is to create dominant dwelling thoughts through ignoring doubts and the wandering away of the mind into old habitual thoughts and beliefs. These new dominant thoughts can be achieved instantly or in minutes, hours, days, weeks, months, years, or decades, or you may even die without achieving them. The time it takes depends on the level of your enlightenment, wisdom, or right-mindedness. Those with right-mindedness or enlightenment can get it instantly in the now or right away. You can repeat the affirmations a thousand times a day, but if you have doubts the other half of the time, then until those doubts are removed, you will not be able to manifest your thoughts.

For example, you came to learn that Santa is not real after you grew up. Your new knowledge is very certain. Your conviction is strong or solid. Next time someone says Santa is real, you will not believe them. You will not doubt your new truth or wisdom, and you do not need to remind yourself this fact or repeat it so as to strengthen your belief or conviction. This conviction came because, as a grown-up, you do not believe any fool will come through your chimney at night and put a present for you under the Christmas tree. This new knowledge, maturity, understanding, truth, and wisdom is not doubtful. Your new wisdom on this particular matter cannot be challenged, changed, or made doubtful. You got this instant and strong conviction instantly at maturity. Here it is your enlightenment but not repetition that brought supremely solid conviction that cannot be challenged or made doubtful. The moment you realize the truth, the old myths got wiped out instantly.

Do your dwelling thoughts create your reality? Yes. Your dwelling thoughts can be conscious or unconscious, and either will create your reality. Just as with your conscious dwelling thoughts, your unconscious dwelling thoughts are infinitely powerful to create your reality. Although your unconscious dwelling thoughts can be seen as repetitions or reaffirmation because you believe and think in terms of your existing limited knowledge, you did not deliberately or consciously repeat those thoughts or beliefs.

Faith is seeing or bringing into existence what you do not see now, such an infinitely powerful gift we all have that does not depend on what you see or the visible world. It is understanding and believing in the invisible or the world within that creates everything and every kind of life for all human beings in this world. Whether you understand it or not, or believe it or not, it is what creates your world.

The subconscious mind creates reality based on your dwelling thoughts (which are the same as your faith). It brings into existence the nonexistent as a result of your dwelling thoughts (faith).

Can a single thought be enough to create your reality without reaffirmation or repetition? Yes. Knowledge of a truth is enough to create your subconscious mind without repetition. Wisdom of the truth becomes your dwelling and dominant thought automatically. Why do some thoughts need to be repeated or reaffirmed? It is because there are other competing thoughts, so you need to make the message clear for the subconscious mind. Therefore, you constantly ignore the wandering thoughts and remind the conscious mind the dominant thoughts or dwelling thoughts that you want to have, and hence create your reality. Let us look at four possible dwelling thoughts and their outcomes in the following scenarios. It's a simplified example for easier understanding.

Scenarios

Scenario 1

Here you have competing thoughts on your mind, but your conscious and deliberate refocusing or dwelling on B will result in reality or manifestation of B.

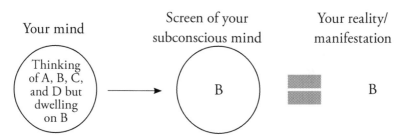

Scenario 2

Here you hope or wish to manifest B, but your dwelling thoughts are on A, C, or D, so you end up manifesting one of them.

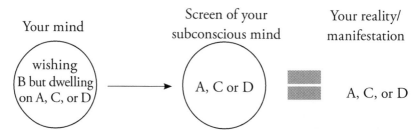

Scenario 3

You have no clear dominant or dwelling thought here; any strong swing to dwell on one of the options could become your reality.

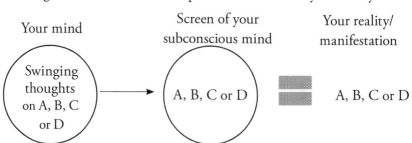

Scenario 4
You don't believe or think of any other alternatives here. You dwell and believe in B as the outcome.

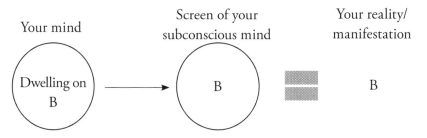

Explanation of the Scenarios

Scenario 1
You have faith in B and repeat (dwell on) it. The outcome will be B. Here the wandering mind is thinking of other possibilities, and the conscious refocusing on B will cost some time and energy. This is doubtful faith, needing purification.

Scenario 2
You consciously reaffirm and repeat B. You want it to happen, but you doubt it is possible. Your thoughts dwell on chances of any of the other three becoming your reality. You want to become a great football player in league 1 of EPL, but you don't believe in yourself or your talent, so you believe that you are only good enough to play in the other leagues. Because of your self-doubt, no matter how many times you repeat that you are going to play for league 1, you will not achieve that. In due time, your doubt will discourage you from repeating or reaffirming these thoughts. So here there is a dwelling thought of not believing in the outcome or its possibility, but at the same time you have hopeful thoughts or wishes. The dwelling thoughts win here (so the dwelling thoughts are your convictions, belief, or faith). The repetition or reaffirmation is the attempt to make one of the possibilities your dwelling thought to create or manifest it in your life.

There is faith here. You believe A, C, or D will happen, and you don't believe B will happen. Either way, you believe in one or the other, whether consciously or deliberately or by default. If you have no faith in B, it means you have faith in all or one of the remaining options. The idea of having no faith at all if you did not have faith in B is wrong. If you believe none of the outcomes are possible, then that is another type of faith. Repetition or reaffirmation cannot be measured or weighed numerically. It is not literally how many times you say what you believe or desire. It is how much time you spend on a particular thought and how strongly you feel about its outcome. To dwell on a certain outcome, you also have to successfully ignore the thoughts of other possible outcomes.

Scenario 3

Unconsciously living, your thoughts swing between health and disease, scarcity and abundance, and other opposing thoughts almost equally here. There is faith and unconscious repetition and reaffirmation of dual/opposing realities. So, the outcome could be any of the four.

Scenario 4

This is a scenario of miracles, infinite power, being one with life, a purified and enlightened soul with right-mindedness. No waste of time (realties do not take time to create), no other choices (certainty, solid or complete faith), no need for repetition or reaffirmation in an attempt to dwell on a particular thought because there is only one thought created by knowledge of the truth or enlightenment. The absence of other possibilities A, C, and D will naturally make B the dwelling or dominant thought. So, reaffirming and repeating B will not make it any clearer or improve the chances of making it a possible outcome; it is the only outcome on your mind.

The fact that you thought or believed Santa was real for the first five to seven years of your life as a child does not mean that you spend another five to seven years of your mature, enlightened adult age reaffirming or repeating your new knowledge or enlightenment to convince yourself that Santa is not real. The simple knowledge of ha-ha, it is a lie is enough to eliminate that ignorance or illusion. The fact that you spent days or years dwelling on certain illusions does not mean you undertake or spend equal or more time to surpass the time spent on old illusions or ignorance so as to make the new wisdom or enlightenment dominant or dwelling. The enlightenment or knowing the truth banishes or eliminates the old illusions or ignorance instantly and thus becomes your new dwelling thought that creates your reality. Truth and illusion cannot coexist. Truth overcomes lies and illusions not by out numbering it or dominating it but by eliminating it instantly, just like light illuminate darkness in instant. Hence, your reality is formed by this new enlightenment naturally and effortlessly. There is nothing you can do about the realities created by the old illusions or lies or ignorance. It is past, and they have already affected your life in one way or another. The same moment you learn the truth, you simultaneously unlearn the old illusions or ignorance. This concept applies in all cases of eliminating the past egoistic thoughts, beliefs, opinions, and identities.

Hope and Faith

Let your hope become your faith and conviction. Hope is the next best thing to faith. But it is just too weak and is only important for those with wishful thinking and doubtful faith. Hope is a doubtful faith. It is just like a wish and not dependable, though it is better than believing you do not have faith at all. It is half faith, thus not strong enough to change your realities. You may live hoping that something good will happen for you in the future, and you may end up not seeing that future or realize your hope. But nothing stands in the way of faith. Faith is now, faith is infinitely powerful, and faith is hope with all the doubts removed. Faith creates the visible world; it is a medium of creation for the infinite intelligence within. Your faith can make anything happen, right now. You don't create or remove faith, but you can veil it with illusions and doubts.

Hope is in the future. It can lead to anxiety and waste of the present moment or the now. Hope means you are doubtful, wishful, and expecting something to happen in the future, while faith means you believe you have received whatever you prayed for.

Naturally, other people can never share or understand your faith. Although the power of faith is equal in everyone, the level of veil and purpose of each person is different. Therefore, it is only natural that people don't understand or measure your faith. They only understand and measure the manifestations (outcome) of your faith, and most would attribute those manifestations to intelligence, luck, past, skills, talent, race, family, education, and so on. All these are the mediums through which faith can manifest. Without faith, no successes or failures are possible.

Faith without action is un-manifested faith. You have to work for and create the right environment for faith to manifest in your life. You can waste the power of your faith through ignorance, doubt, and lack of action among other things. Use the power of faith to create any kind of life and success you choose. You cannot blame your failures on other people and attribute your success to yourself at the same time; you should take responsibility for both. You may blame your failure on your race or origin, birth place, or other conditions in the external environment, but you will find that there are many people who achieved success in those same external environments. You will also find people who failed despite having what others consider a perfect environment, such as a rich family, country, or education. You will find those who have failed to achieve financial success, a happy life, or great careers. You can have the best education or degrees and still feel and live as a failure and unfulfilled. You cannot choose or be held responsible for other people's action, but you are responsible for the type of reaction or responses you choose. You can choose to grow stronger and wiser from those experiences or you can choose to let the experience make you miserable and weak.

When you set alternative goals or dreams to achieve in your life by contemplating, "If goal A fails, I will try goal B," it means you doubt that A will be possible or achieved, and so you have B or other goals in the back of your mind. If you doubt A, then you will fail to achieve or manifest it in your life. Sometimes we waste our time and energy by wishing to manifest A while at the same time having complete faith in B as the outcome. As faith is stronger than a wish, you would consequently manifest B. If you doubt A and B, then both will fail to manifest in your life. If you have complete faith in the possibility of any of the two happening, A or B, then that is what you will get, but in this case, you are not consciously in charge of the exact outcome. You accepted any of those chances as your realities.

If you have no faith in the manifestation of a particular goal in your life, then it is better not to undertake it. You will just waste your time and energy.

If you are hopeful that a particular goal will manifest in your life, then don't be discouraged to undertake or start working on the goal. You will discover the power of your faith, and you will strengthen your conviction along the way.

If you have complete faith in manifestation of a particular goal, no matter how astronomical or impossible it seems to others, consider it achieved. Start working or keep working on those goals without tire or delay. Remember, you don't need and should not expect the consensus or approval of others. Only your faith or belief is needed for the manifestations of those goals, not the faith or beliefs of other people. Only you can choose the level of influence other people's faith, opinions, or beliefs have on your goals. To achieve astronomical success in life, you should completely ignore the opinions and beliefs others have about you. You can see and experience the infinite intelligence and power of your faith only when you learn to ignore what others think of you. This means complete removal of the veils that covered the power of your faith. Here, your responsibility is not to create or strengthen your faith but to remove the veils or illusions. Faith has always been there and has always been infinitely powerful.

When you write down your dreams and goals next time, have absolute faith and conviction to guarantee the outcome and also save your time and energy. Have one great plan and have absolute faith in only one possible outcome. Nothing and no one can and will stop you from achieving your goals. If you don't want the opinions of others, do not share with them your supreme goals. This is not because they are bad people, but it is because they believe that great things or supreme success can only be achieved by certain deserving people but not an average person like you with an imperfect external environment and past. They will only project opinions and beliefs they hold within regarding their limitations and boundaries of success. So, don't be discouraged, perturbed, surprised, or hurt by their opinions.

If you want to operate from a position of power and flow with the current of life, then only value your own opinion and faith. That is universal law and wisdom. Others will only witness the manifestation of your faith and beliefs through your work, which is guaranteed if you believe no other outcome is possible and that no dream is impossible.

You cannot find power or success in illusions or others' opinions. Nothing they say or do will make you powerful or enable you to achieve your supreme dreams or goals. Their approval or words of encouragement are as useless as their disapproval and words of discouragement. Do not seek power in weakness, such as in another person's opinion. As well, you cannot find weakness and failure as a result of valuing your opinion and convictions. Nothing others say or do will make you weak or prevent you from achieving your supreme goals or dreams. Your success, power, and happiness are guaranteed because they come from within and do not depend on other people's opinions or approval. Therefore, you get certainty, peace of mind, self-assurance, self-belief, and stability, while seeking external approval leads to a life of uncertainty, self-doubt, perturbation, and instability.

Faith but Not Strength

I was reading about Anthony Joshua against Charles Martin in the world heavyweight champion boxing fight. Martin, who is defending the belt, looks slim and out of shape physically. I think I have better biceps and muscles than the defending champion. Then I remembered: champions are made out of faith, not muscles. Muhammad Ali was physically small compared to most of his opponents, but it was his faith that made him a champion. They were many black, brown, and white men who were stronger and fitter than Ali at the time, but they did nothing with their strength or muscles, as they did not have strong beliefs in what they could achieve. But it was Ali, the small guy with the supreme belief, that became the champion. All those strong people are dead now, with all the strengths and muscles they had. They could have been champions. It is not even talent that matters but only the belief that you can do it. Then the talent will definitely follow.

One day in the future, on my deathbed, I will look back at my life and say, "What did I do with this beautiful gift?" I will not hold back my unique gift and talent from the world. I have absolute faith in my abilities.

Just like Muhammad Ali, they are so many people with better command of the English language than me, but that does not mean they are using it to share their ideas or intuitions. I will make my unique contribution to the world. They will definitely hear from me.

Muhammed Ali was not the strongest boxer, but he was the greatest world champion.

Ford was not even an engineer but built the first cars. You can mention many others, like Thomas Edison and the Wright brothers.

You can list the greatest people in modern times and the past, and one thing they all have in common is they didn't have the conventional qualifications needed to become the greatest, but they had extraordinary belief in themselves. With that kind of belief, they were guided by their faith to achieve great things in life. The right faith formed through belief and trust in the infinite will lead you to a life of great abundance and success.

Half of Americans Have a Better Voice

Half of Americans have a better voice than one of my favorite rappers, but it is he who is at the top, not the many people who have a better voice. This is another example that explains that your natural skills are less important compared to your beliefs, courage, and confidence. It is more important to have belief, courage, and confidence than natural skills that you never use. The 99 percent of people with the natural skills get nowhere in life, and their skills are wasted, ignored, or never discovered, and they end up not sharing these skills due to lack of belief in themselves and their abilities. And 100 percent of the people with no special skills but with supreme belief, courage, and confidence succeed in whatever field they choose because of their right faith. It shows that faith, not skills or ability, is the driving force behind success.

The Power of the Healed

When I see people getting healed by religious healers like Benny Hinn and Memher Girma, I am amazed by the power of faith. The faith of the healed to receive a miracle through the healer enabled the miracle. I watched on YouTube Memher Girma healing people with various life-threatening diseases. These miracles are only possible because of the faith of the healed in the power of the healer, who is perceived to have been chosen by God. It is the faith of the healed but not the healer that made it possible, but would they believe if someone had told them that their own faith healed them? They would be shocked by the amount of power they have within; it is limitless and infinite. We were all endowed with this infinite power at birth, equally. We all have this power, but it is up to each one of us to recognize this power and remove the illusions that veil us from accessing it. We are only limited by our beliefs and imaginations. Imagine that power within yourself that is the same power of faith that helped Albert Einstein discover his equation. Look for the power within, not without.

Change—Getting Rid of Illusions

You do not have to work hard or struggle to live a life of peace and abundance and all the other positive traits you wish to have. You already have these within you. Live consciously by reminding yourself the existence of these positive attitudes and characters are the manifestation of infinite intelligence within you. Observe and ignore the feelings of struggle or doubt during this period of regaining your true positive character. Doubts and struggle will just veil you from the infinite intelligence within and will end up creating an ego that is in constant search for an answer to seemingly endless illusions that make you feel incomplete.

Creating the ego took time as you reinforced the false identity with every illusion that you had and every opinion others expressed to define you. But the removal of the ego or the false identity, the "little poor you" or the "unfulfilled you," doesn't take any time. It can only happen in this present moment or the now. It cannot happen in the future. If you say, "I will tackle these illusions tomorrow at noon," only the dates change, but the fact remains that this mental exercise will take place when that future becomes the present moment or the now. If the medium in this case, the now, is always constant or the same, then why wait for tomorrow or another day that you are not guaranteed to see? Why postpone your illusions, sickness, or pain? You didn't consciously plan to create these illusions. Why do you need to plan or schedule to remove them? We have thousands of illusions; do you need planning and time for each? Your lifetime will not be enough.

The ego will try to tell you that you need time to change, but that will just extend the life of egoistic thoughts or identities. You will be on your deathbed and still thinking, *I am not there yet*, or *I wish I had the time to do this and that to live a fulfilled life*. No time is enough, and no time is needed for you to change. You don't fight the darkness; instead you switch on the light, and it will be gone. As well, you don't fight or struggle to change the ego; instead, just shrug off the thoughts. If you don't like who you are right now, then you will never like who you will be in the future. There is nothing wrong with you; the negative self-image was created by the ego through unconscious life. Your birth was not a mistake, so learn to love yourself now, with all your imperfections. Love your lot in life and your experiences and your past. Accept your existence as you are now and your circumstances, as if you prayed all your life for it to happen this way. Admire, congratulate, compliment, praise, and adore yourself, and you will have the eyes to see all your blessings and goodness you never recognized before. Don't allow the ego to blind you from seeing the beauty of life and your beauty. The thought of needing more time is the ego's illusion of wasting away your life. Don't be fooled again.

At the beginning of this change, the past illusions of the egoistic identity may pop up in your mind time to time. Don't feel that you failed when your mind wanders away and goes to the past habits of thoughts. This is just natural. Do not let the ego fool you into thinking that you are the same person as in the past. Instead, again and again observe the ego and shine the light of consciousness on it, and the darkness will disappear. You cannot waste your time analyzing every single thought that comes to your mind.

The level of our unacceptance of our life determines the level of our happiness and peace of mind. On the extreme side, you will have people who have refused to accept their situation or something that happened in their life, and they continue living in denial and discontentment. Your complete acceptance of who you are and your life situations will expand your horizon and open your eyes to many possibilities of improving your circumstances, leading you to a life of eternal tranquility.

Remove the doubts and fears that have been keeping you away from living a life of abundance. Stop believing in illusions and open your eyes to this reality—that there is infinite intelligence and power within you. That is the reality most people find it difficult to see, as they grew up listening to and believing the opinion of others regarding their limitations. Your power and genius are infinite. Nothing in this world is too big and too difficult for the infinite intelligence. The thoughts of limitations, scarcity, and difficulty are the thoughts of the ego. I knew and believed in the infinite intelligence within me that can supply me with unlimited wisdom and intuitions every day, and this book is a proof. I never had to worry where my ideas would come from or my vocabulary. Deep within, I knew and believed the infinite intelligence would never fail me. I can only fail if I doubt the existence of infinite intelligence within me and dwell on a mental self-image of scarcity or limited talent or writing skill.

It does not need searching or seeking, and you cannot certainly get it through reading or meditation, as the reading will only point you in the right direction, and the meditation will only provide you with a better mind-set or environment and many other advantages. It is not outside of you; you can only find these answers within you. You cannot get it from my poems or essays. These are all guide books. Just like a map, any teacher will just tell you where you can find it. But you have to walk, fly, or drive there. You can only get it by experiencing and living the journey. Live that life you have always sought. Knowing or reading about it means nothing if you don't live it. Then you will see the amazing work of infinite intelligence in your life.

Let the universe reveal itself to you. And this can only happen by realizing that it has already happened now. The present time is the only point through which you can experience this. Just realize that you have already reached the destiny and goal that you have been seeking. Let not the ego fool you into thinking that it will be another time or another day. This experience does not depend on time; it depends on nothing external. Don't wait until you get your act together or become a better person. It does not require you to change your lifestyle. Just accept it and experience it now, and everything else will follow, whether that is becoming a better you, getting richer, happiness, peace, or anything you have been looking for in life. What the conventional world sees as a failure is just an illusion. There is no failure in the kingdom of God. No one is a failure to God; how can God fail? What is impossible to God? The egoistic mind will try to complicate salvation by analyzing the ways and means of getting there, but the truth tells you that you are already there. The egoistic mind thinks of the preparation, steps, and preconditions to receive salvation at a time in the future. You will never prepare or become holy enough to receive salvation. Think of salvation as the breath you take in and out. Were you given the breath based on your work or status or spiritual purity?

Two Weeks of Diet and Change

I watched for a few minutes a documentary on how just two weeks of a different diet could have a significant impact on our possibility of getting colon cancer. For only two weeks, the food South Africans and African Americans eat were exchanged. The result was astounding. For the two weeks the Africans ate the American food, the probability of getting cancer significantly increased. Also, as a result of eating African food, the probability of getting cancer for the African Americans significantly reduced.

If two weeks of a different diet can result in such a major physiological change, then how much will reading books about philosophy, wisdom, and spiritual teachings change your life and perception? There is no question about the significant and irreversible impact on your life.

Both groups in the dietary experiment experienced significant change because of the changes in their diet for two weeks. But the changes are not obvious to other people who work or live with the experiment group or even to themselves, because it is impossible for anyone to physically see what is happening within their body. The fact that they didn't see the changes does not mean that they did not take place.

It is nature's nature to change; everything is changing around us constantly, every second. We are changing every second. Let not the egoistic mind fool you that you are the same person and that you have not changed just because the changes are not visible to the naked eye. Change is a must and is naturally taking place within you and around you, whether you like it or not, whether you believe it or not.

The biggest changes that are taking within us and around us are the ones that are not visible to the naked eye; you need spiritual eyes or wisdom to see them. Just the same way, only an infinitesimal portion of the universe is visible to our naked eye, whereas the infinite universe is out of our sight. The changes that are taking place within us, mentally, physiologically, and spiritually, are invisible and are infinite and are taking place every second.

The person you were a few days or years ago is totally different from the person you are right now. But because we are accustomed to believing in changes that are visible to our eyes, we are unaware of the infinite changes taking place within us and therefore do not recognize them. The fact that you don't see the rest of the universe does not mean that it does not exist. The fact that you don't see the infinite intelligence doesn't mean it doesn't exist.

The part of the world and the changes that we see are insignificantly small or are the tiniest. The biggest changes and the biggest world are the ones that you don't see. Everything you read and watch and learn is changing you significantly, more than you can ever understand or estimate.

The changes have taken place, but the unconscious mind, or the ego, clinging to the past identity that was created through past references creates an illusion of constancy and permanence that does not exist and cannot exist in reality. Because you don't know this truth, you live in the illusion of an unchanging world that seemed to seal your fate and personality. It is not hard to change; change is natural and taking place all the time involuntarily. What is hard is recognizing the illusion and lies that make it difficult for us to see and accept these changes.

The ego underestimates changes taking place in you because it is fearful of losing its identity and desperately clings to past opinions of the self that were formed through referencing past experiences and opinions.

I read in the news about a scientific report that stipulated the existence of over two trillion galaxies in the universe. Each galaxy has billions of stars. Our sun is one of the billions of stars in our galaxy, and each are thousands of times bigger than the earth. This gives us some perspective of how really small our earth is; it's like a tiny drop of water in an ocean. That is how small we are. In one of the National Geographic documentaries, I heard the scientist say that there are more stars in the universe than the number of sands in this world. Then what is big? Philosophically, big is your own worldview, beliefs, and faith; anything outside you is insignificant and secondary. Your own perspective and beliefs create your reality and world. All you have to take care of are your philosophies and principles of life, your spiritual world, for the invisible world creates your visible world.

What Does the Revelation of Invisible Change Mean?

The revelation about the invisible change means everything. It means that all the spiritual, intellectual, and behavioral changes that you have been working on are taking place within, and all you need is to recognize and believe in them. It means the ego was trying delay the time it took for you to change through illusions of a time in the future when those changes would take place. But you need no time to change; the changes will take place the instant you recognize and believe in them. Your realization and conviction decide how fast the changes take place within. If you believe the changes will take place right in this moment, then they will take place right now. If you believe the changes will take place sometimes in the future, then the changes will take place at a time set by your belief and conviction. In most cases, the invisible change had already taken place within you a long time ago, but the ego's illusions and psychological time delayed the recognition and realization of the changes that took place. In the invisible world, you are a new person now, and you will be a new person tomorrow. You are not the same person at any one moment in life; whether you accept it or not, changes are taking place within you. It means you are already the person you were aspiring to become. There is no need for time or a psychological barrier to make it happen; it has already happened. The people who were healed by their spiritual leaders experienced this miracle because of their faith. They had conviction and belief that they would get healed right then. If you believe the change in you will take place now, then it will take place now. You decide the kind of changes and the time it takes through your belief. You already have within you the power to change your circumstances and life instantly. Do not waste your time and life waiting.

In the Bible (Mark 11:24 New International Version), Jesus said, "Therefore I tell you, whatever you ask for in prayer, believe that you have received it, and it will be yours." He knew the truth and lived by this eternal truth. He did not say, believe that it will happen in the future or tomorrow but believe that it has happened already. This is the power of infinite intelligence within us. You don't need scheduled time, preparation, or plans for it to happen. Simply believe that it has already happened, and you will experience amazing miracles.

The physical reality that people see is just the tiniest result of the infinite reality that has already taken place within you invisibly. But because people are limited to believing only what they see, they are not aware of the changes that have already taken place within them through infinite invincible changes by infinite intelligence within. Whatever you thought of or dreamed of is already a reality in the invisible world. Whatever you pray for, believe that it has happened or as received.

Being Yourself and Conformity

9

The Best Person You Can Imitate

The best person you can imitate in this world is you.
The best speaker you can imitate is you.
The best leader you can imitate is you.
The best spiritual person you can imitate is you.
The most confident person you can imitate is you.
The most intelligent person you can imitate is you.
The best talent you can imitate is yours.
The most courageous person you can imitate is you.

The world has been telling you
You have to look, think, and live like someone else,
Hence killing your unique contributions and talents.
It is like killing you to have more of the other person.
This will invariably fail, as you cannot be her or him.
Just as your fingerprint is unique, so is your talent.
Are you not worthy to live as you are and play your part?
Are you not worthy to make your unique contributions?
Why are you ignoring your true callings?

Enoch Mamo

There is no other person like you in this world
And will never be and has never been, so listen to your heart.
You are here in this world as a vessel to communicate
And share the poems and songs in your heart
That you have been blessed with since birth.
Only then can your intelligence and power be infinite.

Do not try to live somebody else's life.
Live your life as it is, and you will get wise.
No poet will write like me or live like me
Or has same perspective or views as me.
Nor will they have the same life experiences as mine.
I am the only one, will be the only one, and there was no other like
me in the past.
It is better to fail as I am than succeed as somebody else.
That is the meaning of living a true life.
When you learn to value your unique gift,
Only then you will come to see the truth,
That you are the very dream you have been seeking,
And you have all the blessings you have been searching for.

Life is not fair because you have not been fair to yourself.
How can you try to kill who you are, to become somebody else?
Of course, you will fail at this attempt.
And of course it will not be fair in the end.
Above all, you will not be fair to the world
Because your unique talent was killed and buried
The moment you chose imitate.

You can never be another.
The other is already making and has made
His or her unique contribution to this world.
So, make your own for heaven's sake.

I became the best person I can imitate
Only when I accepted myself, and with that I am content.

FUTILE IMITATION

You see Jay Z, Tupac, Obama, Martin Luther King, Steve Jobs, Messi or any other person/persons that you pictured in your mind as representation of success, symbol of success, expression of success etc. The problem is not that they are not successful, the problem is, you are trying to imitate their success by trying to talk, act, behave, dress and live like them, trying to imitate their mannerism and life style to convince yourself and see yourself as successful. Thus, you are veiling, ignoring, undermining and losing the ability of discovering your true identity and potential because you are always trying to become someone else. The focus of your energy and time trying to become someone else will prevent you from living as yourself and hence you will be unable to tap into your unique talent through the unique infinite power and gifts, the focus becomes imitation rather than finding your own success. These thoughts will also make you live in perpetual state of lack, scarcity and discontent. You can never be them or live like them, you will forever say; I don't still talk or act like them, live like them, accumulate wealth or become famous like them, I am not still confident, courageous or talented like them etc. things to imitate from them to reproduce/copy their level of success and lifestyle are infinite, just like your miseries of trying to imitate them are infinite.

> Your success will come through your own unique gifts, power, talents, thoughts, experience, mannerism, lifestyle, tone of voice, temperament, identity, conditions, circumstances, events, environment and time. what is holding you back from seeing and recognizing and appreciating your success is because you are not even looking at it or paying attention as you are stretching your neck

to look at another person's success. You have set a ceiling for yourself of reaching their level of success and trying to fit your success into a shape and form they already set for themselves (you have boxed yourself). You cannot see yourself, you can only see others. Release your perceptions and images of them and focus on yours, comeback to yourself and appreciate and value your mannerism, lifestyle, your own form of confidence, courage and talent and skills, see them as uniquely yours' and the way you exist. Love and express yourself as you can only love and express yourself. You will then clearly see yourself and your unique gifts and power. And only then, will you have the wisdom and eyes to see that you are a success already. Not accepting your unique gifts and existence, is like a cat trying to bark and walk like a dog because the cat thinks the dog's life is better so it tried to be a dog. You know it will never succeed, so will your attempt to imitate others.

Accepting yourself is truly loving yourself, that is true gratitude, that is true success, power, intelligence, wealth and treasure. In the past, you thought you lacked them, because of your wrong/ignorant perception that they can be expressed or manifested only in certain way/ the ways other people you are trying to imitate expressed those unique talents and success. You thought success or confidence or wealth can only be expressed in a certain way, life style, mannerism, talk, ways of meditating etc. It is like you are saying, you recognize water if it is only given to you in a specific shape and color of glass.

If it is given to you in a plastic metallic or ceramic container, then you say that it is not water.

Just like everyone, Bezos is not wealthy because of how much money he has, his true wealth is the unique talent/ideas he had that he shared with the world. The money/financial wealth is the by-product of the true/real wealth we have within. that true wealth can be manifested or have unlimited types of by-products, the by-products can have a common scale or unit of measurement but not the true/real wealth (the product itself or the source), selling oranges in the market is not the only way of making money. Accept your peace, accept your wealth/treasures to get wealth/treasures, accept your confidence to be confident, accept your talent to have talents, accept your intelligence, to have intelligence. Just like everybody, you have them, but the way you manifest or express them is uniquely yours'. We all have abundant intelligence, power, talents, treasures, wealth, confidence, and courage within us. Their expression/manifestations are different and unique to each of us. Your lack comes when you try to imitate the unique expression or manifestation of others and ignore yours'. Here, you are abandoning what you have in order to seek what you don't have and cannot have, therefore, no wonder you always feel lack. You will always feel like a failure, incomplete, or having less, because your measure of success is how good you imitated the unique manifestation/expression of others. You will always fail to be them. You tried to express your confidence like a person you were trying to imitate, then you start thinking you don't have confidence because you cannot express it like that person (as expected in every case of imitation). What you failed at or lacked is not confidence but the attempt to express your confidence in a manner or unique ways the person you were trying to imitate expressed, that was a natural and guaranteed failure.

Once you recognize the images of others expression/ manifestation of success you were trying to imitate, replace them with your positive self image created in your invisible world, then they will manifest. Consciously create your positive self-image by using your own; tone of voice, mannerism, smile and gestures to create your unique manifestations or expression of the infinite intelligence, power, confidence and wealth, treasures within you. Don't try to copy or imitate the expression of others, when it comes to your mind, treat it as wondering away of the mind. Accept that you have all those infinite gifts/abundance/ intelligence and others blessings, that you withheld from yourself before by trying to copy others, now all those illusions have gone and you just express those gifts/blessings in your own way.

Before you struggled to walk or could not walk properly not because there is something wrong with your legs or you didn't have good legs, but it was because you were trying hard to exactly copy the walking style of others. Sometimes, you try to copy different people's walking style each new day, such that you have no idea, if you have your own unique walking style. You see, when you stop trying to imitate others, you will have the time or insight to see your gifts/blessings and you become more grateful for what you have. You will have the chance to live truly as yourself. All the search and journey lead you back to yourself. Now I understand how we were able to create these astronomical innovations and abundance as humans, because each expressed their unique gifts and changed the world in their own way. Those who lived their lives trying to imitate others, wasted their lives on discontent, mediocrity, scarcity, lack, confusion in unacceptance of their time and unique gifts.

When you stop imitating and instead accept your unique gifts/talents/ways of expression or manifestation, then you will start appreciating your intuitions, instincts, opinions, decisions, life-style, conditions, past, present, family and talents. You will take yourself and your life seriously and love yourself and have supreme confidence. No matter how long and how hard the cat tries to be a dog, it will never be a dog. Corporations and education system try to teach you how to imitate others success or lifestyle or expression. Walk out of this madness.

FINDING YOUR TALENT

Why are you seeing yourself as imperfect and scarcely talented? why are you denying yourself and withholding your unique gifts through thoughts of limitation and scarcity? Forget the past, nobody is denying those thoughts, nobody is thinking for you on your behalf. You have 100% unrestricted free will to think of yourself as having abundant intelligence, talent, skills, power and health right now. Who and what are preventing you from having these thoughts now? Forget the self-limiting thoughts you used to have in the past, welcome the miracles of the infinite intelligence in your life. Treat all the past self-limiting thoughts as wondering away of the mind. Remember the past has no power over you, it is you who is giving this power to the past by thinking of it in this present moment, otherwise the past has no life at all, it is dead but the ego made you believe that it is real and alive and powerful to shape your present and future. Everyday, do a simple experiment of consciously ignoring the past self-limiting thoughts you had and replace them with a new thought of having abundant intelligence, talents, power and good health and then you will soon see in your life the manifestations of these new positive thoughts. Right-mindedness includes the absolute rejection and ignoring of the past self-limiting thoughts and identities. The only real and powerful self-image is the self-image you are creating right now consciously. It is your responsibility to search for that unique talent or gift you have within you and express and share it with others to change the world. That unique talent becomes your purpose and gift you give to the world. You will dazzle beyond measure.

What makes people not discover their unique talents?

- The education system that produces mass future employees for corporates. There are millions of people with similar degrees etc.
- Life's daily demand and expectations. Most people do not have the time to look within and find their unique talents. The conventional wisdom and expectation is, finish school, find work, marry, have children, retire and then die. So, our career plans and choices are shaped by traditions, others opinion and expectations.
- Fear of experiencing your unique talent getting rejected, ridiculed and criticized by others. Fear of offending others and challenging the status quo. Also, some fear getting labelled as crazy, awkward, misfit etc.
- Most people are also motivated by financial gain and income security. They are afraid of risking their time and

energy on searching for their unique talent. Therefore, they find it easier and safer to follow conventional wisdom and expectation. They study IT or Engineering because there demands for those types of skills, hence they can easily find a job. Sometimes it is a failure at something that will unconsciously lead you to discovering your unique talent or genius, then you become conscious of your gifts and naturally fall in love with it. But, there are others who consciously look for their unique talent or genius.

- For some, their parents or teachers chose for them what career path to follow. Their parents or relatives find them a job and they easily settle in life. So, why hustle trying to look within for their unique talents or genius? So, you thought people were doing you a favor or you thought you had an advantage over others who didn't have good network like you? But the reality is you are at disadvantage, as you didn't have the time or chance of looking within for your unique talent.

Modern Education System and Worship of Mentors

The education system is really messed up and wasting the lives of people more than all the drugs combined. It is wasting the talent and time of many intelligent people. The addiction to education is as dangerous as any other addictions known to humans. Little education is much better than a lot of formal education. The feeling of chronic unfulfillment that you try to quench through getting one more degree or one more certificate to meet the needs of your future employer is so dangerous, toxic, and life corroding. You waste your very life by pursuing the need to impress your potential future employer.

The other problem with education is its ability to destroy the unique talents and independent thoughts of most people. The systematic factory-like production of a disciplined work force that has forsaken its individual identity and replaced it with institutional or corporate identity is one of the biggest failures of our modern education system.

The learners have lost themselves and have become timid and apologetic for an offer of meager earnings and mediocre work that they sacrificed their whole life for. Students have become worshippers of their past and a few people who they were taught to believe should be their role models to imitate. This resulted in the death of their unique gifts as they surrendered to worship the achievements of others, hence foregoing their own contributions to this world. Little do they know that they are as much gifted as the people they admire. The habit of reading, learning, and quoting others' wisdom has made them ignore their own intuitions and opinions. Moreover, the habit of learning from others has led them to waste their life through attempts of imitation. You are your own portion; you can wait for a trillion of years, but no one like you will be born, and you will never become like any other person in this world. You are your own man or woman.

The other side effect of education is the production of perpetual listeners. These are individuals who prefer to listen to others rather than listen to themselves. For them, their truth is not truth unless they get others' approval, and they believe that truth can only be learned and is not something that exists within them. These are individuals who are always eager to conform to please others in order to keep the peace and the status quo. These are people who are ashamed of their ideas and creativity and adopt the ideas of others. Their aim in life is just to look like everybody else. They have lost their souls. In this attempt, they fail to live truly as themselves and invariably fail to live like others through imitation. The freedom of speech we proclaim to have is nothing but an illusion if we cannot express our creativity and unique ideas. The conventional freedom in reality is the freedom of talking and speaking like others with whom you share the same ideas, out of the need to belong to a group rather than express your own ideas.

If we all lived like the others, with uniformly acquired knowledge that is not original, if not for the few braves who realized their individual genius, we would not have any new inventions, any new schools of thought, no new scientific breakthroughs and discoveries, no religions, no schools, no countries, no music, no industrialization, no computers, no phones, no iPad or tablets, no electricity, no cars, no civilization, no poems ... Nothing. Just a few people who were courageous enough to listen to their intuition and refused to cowardly conform made all these achievements possible. Then how foolish are we to support conformity and punish those who challenge the status quo? All these people who afforded us all the comforts, wisdoms, philosophies, poems, and inventions we enjoy today were misunderstood in their lifetime.

From early on, the modern education system tells you that you are not good enough. Sometimes this sentiment is reinforced by parents. You are taught in school that you have to think and act like someone else. You have to try to become like this or that person or student. The young adult grows up trying to fit in and dreams of looking like others. They are haunted by this perpetual feeling of "I am not good enough" and "I have to make my resume look better by adding more skills, experiences, and education." They are left with more tuition and less intuition. They spend a lifetime chasing the winds.

There is exaggeration of the importance of mentors. That is becoming a willing slave to a master. This is a means by which the modern education system prolongs the student-teacher type of relationship that looks at the student as a human being who is less than the other person and so needs the help of the mentor even after leaving school. No great poet, writer, philosopher, or inventor had a mentor for the whole of their lives. They never lived their lives trying to fit in to someone else's shoes. Living under the shadow of someone else is a sure way of putting a ceiling on your potential, set by the achievement of your mentor, who may not even have your best interest at heart.

More Than Grades

More than grades in school, kids should be brought up in an environment that encourages high self-esteem and confidence. The way kids are treated will determine their success in life more than their grades. If your kids are treated with respect and their independence and confidence are encouraged at early age, then you will have an adult that will become a great leader and succeed in any field.

If you have a kid who is disrespected, mistreated, humiliated, and treated like a fool and good for nothing by either parents or teachers, then you will have a broken and weak adult who becomes dependent on government or other people and achieves almost nothing in life. The only exception here is if the adult grows up to use the negative childhood experience for his or her enlightenment and spiritual growth.

Being a Success as Yourself

When you stop trying to be someone else, the forces of nature are with you. As the current of the river carries the log effortlessly down the stream, you will flow with the forces of nature. All things come your way to build you supremely, whether those things are considered good or bad in the eyes of other people.

The moment you try to become like everybody else, you lose your true freedom and worth. You try to speak like so and so. How can you forsake your life and self-worth to become another? I worked as a teller for a bank. It was shame to see and experience the managers trying to make everyone act and speak in the same manner. Everybody greets you using the exact same sentences and words every day. I came to learn how corporates kill creativity and dehumanize their employees. No one should be subjected to systematic abuse.

Life's Equation

One afternoon, I was thinking of an imbalanced and distorted life's equation, which is very hypothetical and qualitative. It is not even an equation, as both sides do not balance, but I was having this particular thought in terms of an equation. I was thinking on one side of the equation, you have you, which includes the infinite intelligence in you and your time, the opinions you have of yourself, your personality, and so on. On the other side of the equation, you have other people's opinions of you, the time you spend processing your thoughts or intuitions influenced by others, the thoughts you have about other people, the time you spend reading about or watching other people's lives, the time you spend processing outside information, the time you spend trying to look and live like other people, and so on.

You can simply put the equation as: real (primary) world on one side of the equation, and on the other side of the equation, you have the external (secondary) world. These two sides of the equation will never balance. You should give minimal weight to the outside or external world and spend all your worldly life and time paying attention to the real, inside, primary world. If you stick to this simple philosophy in life, you will realize how easy it is to become yourself. You will not waste your time and energy on the "external world" side of the equation.

Your internal reality will create your external reality. You must create it, believe it, and see it in your own internal world before other people can see. What I am thinking right now, what I am doing right now, the way I do things and my philosophies in life are unique to me, and no one can recreate my life. Then why should I try to recreate someone else's life? No matter how good and successful the other person's life is or was, I cannot recreate it. In addition to wasting my time and energy, the attempt will make me ignore my intuition and talent. That is how most people end up with perpetual discontent and a sense of failure, because they cannot replicate the life of another person, and they abandoned their own lives as a result of the attempt. You will get the same result of failure and discontentment if you continue comparing yourself to another person in terms of wealth, health, social status, lifestyle, life experience, spiritual growth, physical appearance, career growth, unique talent or gift or skills, and emotional and cognitive IQ. Live and love your life. It is the only way you can discover the infinite intelligence and treasures within to live a happy, healthy, contented life with abundant wealth and dazzling, unique talents or skills. Every time the mind wanders away to think of another person's life, be alert and conscious to refocus back onto your life. Pay minimal attention to the life stories and biographies of other people and instead refocus that energy and time to improve your own life situations and skills.

At this moment, the infinite intelligence is working through me in a unique way, and I am testifying this unique life and talent that I was blessed with. I am not trying to think, speak, or write like someone else. This writing is a piece of me. If I tried to write like someone else, all my ideas would disappear, as I would be abandoning my intuition. If for a single second I have not lived in their world and I cannot imagine a single second of their thoughts, then how can I try to replicate their life? How can I write and think like the other person?

My choice of words and writing skills and styles will be uniquely mine. Trying to compare or write like someone else is a sure way of wasting my life writing a book guaranteed to fail. The way I live, write, and think is perfect because it is uniquely mine, born from my intuitions and life experiences. We should also accept ourselves as we are and see our own uniqueness that makes this world a more beautiful place. The frustrations and limitations come to us because we try to compare ourselves or try to be someone else. Sing the songs in your heart the only way you know and the only way you can. Be content with your songs, styles, and abilities. That is what the world is looking for, and you will be able to tap into the resources of infinite intelligence and talent that already exist within you. Only your own key can open up the doors of these resources, not a copied key. The world is not looking for another Shakespeare or Beyoncé; they each used their own keys to tap into the infinite intelligence and talent within. It is a waste trying to open this door with a copied key that was produced by imitation and comparison.

I have every right to have a bold dream and share my ideas just as anybody else. Dreams are not reserved for a few chosen. My life will prove to others that your bold dreams can come true. There is nothing impossible, and I am blessed to be in this unique position. I am now at the training stage for the Olympics, just like the amazing training of Usain Bolt before he stepped onto the world stage and Olympic podium.

This is Michelangelo's artwork before it was recognizable.

This is Shakespeare's writing before anybody read it.

This is Albert Einstein's equation before it was revealed to the world.

This is a beautiful work of art in the form of philosophy, spiritual teaching, poems, and essays.

After even writing it down several times before, I had to remind myself the measurement for the success of my book by looking at different parameters. The book is already a success, since it has changed my life significantly; any further success is secondary and not as important. I should not think too much about the publishing and public opinion of the book. My focus is the change that is taking place within me. The beautiful ideas that I am writing down supremely inspired me. I will write the book as beautifully as I can for myself. I will learn immensely from the ideas and experience, which will result in astronomical spiritual growth. This is the best experience of my life, so I will enjoy the journey.

Doubt and fear of failure are produced by the thoughts of expecting success in the future. The most important thing is not the goal but the process or the activity. For example, the success of my book only depends upon my everyday writing of the essays and poems. The process is already successful, since the essays and poems have enlightened and changed me for the better, and I am happy expressing these intuitions.

The wisdom that I am gaining through my writing is the most important thing and is a success. The measure of my success is how these truths are changing my world, not any other external world. Every other thing is secondary. The wisdom, belief, courage, confidence, health, happiness, and so many other blessings I gained are invaluable. What worked for me will also work for the rest of the world.

The ego will try to compare you with others professionally—the social status, wealth, education, and career progress. They all mean nothing. Do not compare yourself; that is life wasting.

You should love and accept your past, present, and circumstances. You should embrace your life completely. We all have a unique position and contribution that makes this life more beautiful.

The World Within

People make a lot of mistakes and live a life of fear and other illusions because they think the real world is the external world. They worry about convincing other people or worry about what other people think of them, or they worry about how other people react to this or that action they took. The truth is the real world is the world within, the only opinion that matters is your own opinion, the only reaction that matters is your own, and the only convincing you need is yours. The only true and primary world is the one inside you (your own thoughts). Don't try to live up to the opinions of others. That is the best way to lose yourself, your power, your peace, and even the external world. You lose everything trying to chase the illusion of the external world. Don't try to make it hard and complicated by worrying about the opinions of others. Remember the simple truth: the only world that matters most is yours. It's really simple to remember and follow. All your thoughts and actions should be based on those simple truths, and you will never go wrong.

Looking within and Its Repercussion

We mostly assume that the outcome of looking within means an immediate monetary gain, but the truth is when you search deep inside your soul, what you gain is a great character, spiritual harmony, joy, and peace of mind. This outcome will invariably lead to, among other things, financial gain and better health. You will inherit the kingdom of God first, and the rest will come to you. The spiritual growth and gain within will soon transform your realities and the external world.

A lot of learning that will take place at the beginning of your spiritual journey is to unlearn what you are not. Formal education, others' opinions, and life experiences veiled the true self by moving away from the true treasures and grace you have within in order to seek and depend on the external treasures. The rigorous process of looking within will help you unlearn and remove the egoistic identity that you acquired over the years. Then you will start appreciating and simply valuing your very existence as a human at this time, place, and condition. You will begin to see that your perspective and understanding are creating your world or realities.

Ideas and Talents—They Are Already Within

Ideas for my books are already within me. They will never come from another person, a book, or anything outside me. They will come flowing out from within. They do not need a more perfect place, time, or state of enlightenment. The ideas will come out spontaneously, unannounced. All I have to do is write them down immediately. I am the instrument through which the infinite intelligence expresses the truth.

No altered state of mind to get the ideas but just the realization that God is working in you right now, at this very moment and your life conditions. You do not seek God; he is already within you all the time. You only seek what is outside you. God is within. He cannot come to you or reveal himself to you, because he is already within. You do not need time and effort to find God because he is already within. No one can take that away from you or give it to you. All you have to do is recognize that God is within you all the time and remind yourself of this truth.

The Knowledge of Truth and Its Use

Knowing the truth or reading about it means nothing if you cannot practice it in your daily life. The person who knows the truth and never lives by it is worse than the person who doesn't know the truth. At least one did not waste their precious life learning about truth that they never used.

Nonconformity in the Modern World

How do you then succeed in this modern world that disapproves and crushes nonconformity? Some may see this as a David versus Goliath fight. How do you think differently and still succeed? If you talk, act, and smile like everybody else, then you are everybody. Okay, you can say I am myself when I go home. Does that make you part-time you and part-time everybody else? Or are you trying to act like every other husband or wife even at home? Does being you or maintaining self-identity make you a failure? How do you reconcile individuality and group identity? I remember asking myself these questions out of anger and frustration, which crops up whenever I am doing something that everybody else has not done or may not approve. The anger is because of the probability of rejection as a result challenging the status quo or conventional wisdom. This is truly a unique life path I am supremely enjoying. There is no turning back now. I cannot fail to live as I am, so I am already who I am. There is no attempt of trying to become someone else or replicate someone else's success or lifestyle. I have already arrived. There is no becoming, no seeking fulfillment in the future, no comparisons, and so no possibility of failure.

Focusing on Past Teachings

Why should I care about the great poets who lived before me? I am contented and happy with the skills that I have. I respect the past poets, but I blossom where I am planted. I am the poet and a writer of my place and time. I was born in this century, in this place and family, and went through this experience to write a poem about it, not a poem about another person's life experience. We should look within, and we will realize that we have enough talents within us. We should stop looking over at our neighbor's work or comparing ourselves with others.

No one star dims its lights to admire the brightness of another star. Why do you dim the light of life in you to admire the life of others? Your life is important to you, just as their lives are important to them. No single soul is better than the other. So why do you hold in awe and admire the life of others while you should be holding in awe and admiring your life more than any other person's in this world? What kind of example are you leaving for your kids and the next generation? Are you teaching them that other people's lives are better than theirs? Better leave them with no single penny of inheritance than make them lose their soul through illusions.

Your life is as important as any other person you can think of in this world. Live your life to the fullest just like the star that you are and let the others live theirs.

We are all capable of achieving the great things in life or reaching goals that seem impossible to others. There is no impossible in this life; anything you believe in and imagine will come true.

Do not worship the past or the present people who you think are great. You are just as great. That is the same belief and confidence we should instill in our kids.

The best poems, essays, and spiritual teachings, wisdoms, and truths are yet to be written. Can you imagine if we were still flying models of the first planes the Wright brothers invented? If we were still using the first phone models Alexander Bell invented or the first cars that Henry Ford invented? Why are we then fixated on the past writings of the sages, poems, and spiritual teachings? We have as much access to infinite intelligence and genius in this century. We have to write down the truths and convictions revealed to us in our everyday lives. We have to write better poems than Shakespeare, Walt Whitman, Hafiz, Rumi, and John Milton. We have to write better spiritual teachings than Buddha, Emerson, and Tao. We have to stop worshiping the past and reinterpreting their works and quoting them every day. Dwelling on those past teachings and sages is taking away our life's force and time, just like any other contemporary consumerism or materialism that disintegrates our whole self and harmony and make us move away from the infinite intelligence within us. The past teachers are not any better than us. Why are we putting ourselves below them? Why should we live under their shadows? If they had the power to come back and say something to us, I believe they would tell us to let go of the idol worshipping. Just as we say, "The best is yet to come," we should say the same about poems, spiritual teachings, and philosophies of life. Let our teachings reflect our current realities and lifestyles. Let the future generations write better poems and philosophies than we do. Why do we insist on living in the modern world and sticking to old teachings? Just like science, we should strive to find new spiritual teachings and better poems. If our spiritual teachings do not stand the test of time, then let them be shredded and replaced with new ones.

You can be as great as any of our inventors, writers, or spiritual teachers of the past. It is already in you; stop the search and start living your dreams. You have the same infinite intelligence as they did, not any less and not any more. We are all born with the same infinite intelligence and genius within. They did not acquire it, and you certainly will not. You just need to remove the illusion that has covered it; then it will flow out. Remove all the fake identities that you have given yourself or others gave you in the past.

Then you will realize that you have everything and that you can achieve anything.

The most important thing is not what others tell you or what you tell others; it is what you tell yourself.

No Writer Is Made in a Classroom

No great writer is made in a classroom or Ivy League college. True writers are made by their experiences of life and their ability to express their intuitions. The classroom produces uniform people who act and think alike, and therefore, most have no different stories to tell. They do not have their own truths or opinions but conform to a uniform style of writing and ideas they learnt in class.

Nonconformist

If I decided writing a book is a good thing, it does not matter what others think of my career moves. I go ahead 100 percent and do it. I will continue with the project with the whole of my heart. The outcome is not that important to me. The important thing is I am enjoying doing this now. The writing is a form of therapy that is giving me joy, peace, and health; these are the goals of every career and the greatest wealth. It means I have reached the goal of my career; I am already successful since, even in conventional terms, the success of your career is measured using the same parameters. The difference between this project and my past failed career projects is that I am not looking for fulfillment or future success in this project. I am already fulfilled. The journey itself is the fulfillment. I have truly started enjoying life just like sport professionals such as soccer players. You enjoy the game or the process. In this project, failure has 0 percent chance while success is already 100 percent achieved. This project is based on yoga karma. I am not focused on the gold but the alchemy. The process is a success. The outcome is not my business.

Better Comes after Nonconformity

I read a little about the early civil rights activities of Martin Luther King Jr. In 1955, he organized the boycotting of public transportation and represented one of the defendants who defied the segregated public transportation system. If he had not said, "This is not good enough," and conformed, then nothing might have happened, and who knows how many more years the segregation policy could have continued. Every great person's history in this world is a story of nonconformity. If you disagree and demand better, then you will get better. The life of former slave Frederick Douglass, who rose to great fortune and stature in the antislavery struggle, is another example of nonconformity.

Self-Trust

Society has made individuals not trust their own instincts through schools, career expectations, subordination, religion, and other ways. Listen to your intuition more than anybody or anything else in this world. Trust yourself more than anything or anyone else, not even a sage. Listen to that hunch and intuition that comes spontaneously. It is the most intelligent and genius teacher, sage, advisor, and decision-maker in this world for you. Listen and write down the ideas immediately. I stop whatever I am doing and write down my intuitions in a sentence or two as they come.

The Architect

Just like in many other fields, the work of an architect starts with imagination. Then they put the design on paper, and the last product is the physical structure or a building. The structure is based on the imagination of the architect, and they expect other contractors to follow their design. In life, your imagination and dominant habitual thoughts create your reality. When you dwell on certain thoughts all day, you are giving out a design that the infinite intelligence or subconscious mind should follow, just like the contractors. Every thought that you dwell on is designing what kind of life you will live. Remember, it is not what kind of life you wish to live but what kind of life you are guaranteed to live. Your subconscious mind will faithfully deliver the results of your dominant thoughts, whether you chose them consciously or unconsciously.

Some people might ask, "What about those involuntary thoughts that come to mind?" If you acknowledge those thoughts as the wandering mind and ignore them, then they do not count as part of the drawing in your design. They will be erased as quickly as they were sketched, or sometimes they were not sketched at all. For a thought to become part of your design, you have to persistently dwell on it for a significant part of your day or life to see its exact outcome. Consciously or unconsciously, some people dwell on thoughts of fear and scarcity; those thoughts will form their reality. On the other hand, consciously or unconsciously, some people dwell on thoughts of abundance and courage, and those thoughts will end up creating their reality.

Every new discovery, whether in science, art, or literature, starts with imagination. These imaginations only exist only in the mind of the pioneer. The pioneer imagines ideas beyond the boundaries of existing knowledge or status quo and thinks of possibilities of new realities. These possible new realities are not real to the masses and therefore can easily be rejected. The pioneer doesn't ask for a consensus or approval from the masses on what kind of new realities or imagination they should choose to undertake; otherwise we would not have progressed as human beings.

The architect does not stop imagining or drawing their design just because it is not yet a reality to you. They do not need your consent or affirmation that the design is possible. Instead, they start imagining the design, which later becomes a reality to you when you see the final drawing or physical structure. That is the same for any other dream or aspiration you have in your life. If you focus on or are concerned about public opinion or approval, then it becomes impossible to imagine anything new. Worrying about public opinion kills your creativity and locks you within the boundaries of existing knowledge. Imagination is not enough. We have to have strong conviction and courage to share our ideas and bring changes. We have to believe in ourselves and appreciate our unique intuitions and imagination. Do not allow fear of rejection or becoming a misfit to kill your dream of imagining a new and a better world. Do not doubt yourself because people may see you as crazy or strange. You create your own path. You should not limit yourself by following other people's paths or ways of life or their thoughts, beliefs, or value system. Pioneering is the best form of heroism. It takes a great hero to change the world.

Seeking Group Identity

Like many people, I have also sought for group identity in the past. I remember the time I tried to join some spiritual groups in Calgary, and I also thought of becoming a member of a church in the past. That was an attempt by the ego to seek its identity outside instead of inside. This was because the ego feels incomplete and seeks a sense of fulfillment and completeness by joining a larger group. The other illusion is the ego's need to conform and attempt to look like other people in your surroundings.

The attempt to please others results in contempt from others and by self to self. If you do not respect yourself enough to appreciate, accept, and be proud and happy about yourself, then how do you expect others to respect you? You should celebrate, appreciate, and be respectful of your uniqueness and portion. If you do not respect that, then how do you expect others to respect you? If you do not respect yourself, it is obvious that others will not respect you.

You have to give the highest respect to who you are—your beliefs, principles, background, skills, abilities, opinions, choices in life, styles, look, color, family, education, background, ethnicity, and career—so that others will respect you too. You should not fall for the lie that regards the culture and lifestyle of others as better than yours. Just like two different flowers blossom side by side, you should blossom without trying to become another. That does not mean despising or disrespecting others' culture. The fact that you love your kids does not mean you hate other people's kids. The more you love and respect your kids, the more you love and respect other people's kids; it is the same when it comes to the love you have for yourself and who you are.

Respect your life, and others will follow. The same applies for respecting and loving your kids. Stop admiring your neighbors and admire what you have. Be content with what you have and who you are, and you will be the wealthiest and happiest person on earth. Contentment is the greatest wealth you can have on this earth.

That doesn't mean you should not try to improve your life's conditions or make friends; it means be proud and accepting of who you are.

10

Living in the Real World

The moderate wind sways and rustles the branches of a tree but not the roots. The momentary wandering of the mind or the egoistic thoughts are normal, and you should just observe and ignore the negative thoughts or self-talk. Your roots or the inner peace and consciousness can never be uprooted by these temporary negative thoughts or self-talk. You should not get perturbed by these thoughts but remain calm and still. Make your dwelling in this inner peace and consciousness.

Proclamation

When you say you are the greatest, who are you saying it to? Who can stop you if you choose to be the greatest? Nobody can. Nobody can stop you if you truly believe and say you are the greatest. It is also the same when you say that you are a failure or small or insignificant. Nobody can change that feeling or stop you from becoming what you proclaimed. Your world is created by your thoughts but not by circumstances or other beings. You have unlimited power within you to manifest your thoughts and beliefs into reality. That is one of the most powerful tools you have. This is not a secret, this is not the world conspiring, and this is not chance. This is a fact and a reality of life. When you decide to do something, all the forces or energies of the universe will be at your service to make your proclamations and beliefs a reality; they are just waiting for your command.

When you say you are the greatest, you are referring to the power of the infinite intelligence within you. You have to remind yourself of these qualities and powers in you, and soon it will be the external reality. You are the master of your world, and you are in control of your destiny. No circumstance or human can stand in your way.

Giving up Searching and Seeking

When you give up seeking, you will find all the answers. Most of the time, your seeking is like looking for a torch that is in your hand, like a friend of mine did when I was in a boarding school. You are mostly searching for what you already have within. When you stop searching, you realize your own uniqueness that shines for the world. You are the sun, and in comparison, what you are searching for is a candlelight. Will you stand outside on a sunny day and light a candle to see more clearly? How can you seek the light of a candle in daylight outside? That is what your seeking of outside treasures and fulfillment represents. You have infinite intelligence within that is the source of everything. When you recognize the eternal light within, then you will dazzle like a star in everything you do. Nothing can stand in your way, because you are the way itself. You are the whole path, and you stretch beyond the obstacles that occupy the tiniest portion of length of the path.

The way of living a settled, content, and fulfilled life is by mentally creating those conditions rather than waiting for external conditions to be perfect. Contentment cannot come from outside through accomplishing certain things in life; you can only find it within yourself. Nature's law will never be broken and cannot work in reverse; you can only break yourself against the laws of nature. If you expect contentment from outside, you will live a life of waiting for something to happen to fulfill you and die without truly living. You will waste your youth and the eternal gift of this life called the present moment.

Just like an architect or a carpenter, create the mental picture first, and then you will see it in the physical world as your reality. Setting an external goal as a condition to feel contentment will postpone your happiness and will gradually develop into a habit. You will continue setting new goals habitually, every time you achieve the old ones. It is like giving to someone who is illiterate a pen and paper to write a sentence. Will you make them write by changing the types or colors of the paper and pen you gave them? Will these changes make any difference, no matter how many times you try? You have to teach them how to write to make them write. And in your case, the ignorance and illusion of discontentment and an unfulfilled life will follow you to your new situation or life until you address the underlying issue. Rid yourself of the illusion and ignorance first, and you will gain fulfillment and happiness instantly through changing your mental picture and perspective, and you will be carried along that health and happiness for life. Just like the literate person will carry their writing skills everywhere and all the time and will be able to write on any type of paper using any color of pen. Heal yourself first. You need no external accomplishment or help or favor to gain that health now. All the power is within you to live a fulfilled, contented, and happy life. You have already wasted so many precious years in the past. Say it is enough now. Don't live your life in waiting. You are not guaranteed tomorrow. Live fully now, this moment, in this situation and this day by removing these illusions but not by trying to change your future goals or aspirations to gain contentment or fulfillment.

Desperation Voted out on X Factor

As it should be, a woman who was on *British X Factor* was voted out from the competition because she was so desperate. Nicole, who is one of the judges on the show, told the contestant, "You should have sung from a place of strength." The woman sounded so desperate and needy. She presented herself as a weak and needy person. You know you will not get grace and respect by disrespecting and disgracing yourself. If you present yourself as weak, needy, desperate, or a victim, the outcome will not be any different from what you thought of yourself. You will reap what you sow.

Desperately clinging to anything in this life is the best way of losing it. Desperation does not make you more deserving but instead will make it impossible for you to get what you are looking for. It will lead you to neglecting and underestimating your most valuable internal treasures, which are the sources of true happiness and fulfillment. When you abandon these internal treasures, failure and discontent are guaranteed.

The desperation will result in stress, neediness, anger, perturbation, dependence, low self-esteem, and lack of self-confidence. Learn to love, appreciate, value, and accept yourself now, before you try to achieve anything external. Remember to fully enjoy the present moment, and remember the present moment is the best and most perfect time of your life. It will teach you not to overvalue the importance of tomorrow or the future or what it will bring.

Listening to the Rain

Driving to work, it was raining.
I turned off the radio to listen
to the raindrops on my car's roof.
A dedication from nature is my latest hip-hop.

I felt calm and peaceful inside,
The raindrops silencing my mind.
The wipers move, dancing to the music.
With the engine roar in the background,
This serendipitous concert
Filled my heart with delight.

Living Like a Powerless Victim

The failure to recognize our power has led us to live like a powerless victim that waits to be hurt by people, things, circumstances, time, and health. We wait and worry that we'll get this or that illness, and when that fear becomes a reality and we get ill, we get overwhelmed by sadness and confusion. But why? All we were thinking of and attracting to ourselves was about getting ill. If you had the power to transmit all your thoughts onto a blank piece of paper in the form of a drawing or a writing, would you be surprised to see the drawings or the writings that were a result of your thoughts?

Nothing bad happens to the sage; everything happens to either enlighten them or make them happy. Where is the loss or what makes them worry? They feast on all experiences. Even those things others see as a loss or a problem, they use for enlightenment.

When the World You Created Looks Imposed

One of the greatest illusions is when you look at the world that you created as a world that is imposed on you. You created every circumstance and experience you are going through, have gone through, and will go through. These are some of the things that are not your creations: the place you were born, you family, your race, and your childhood. But the things you have not created do not determine what you can achieve in life, your possibilities or potential. You have far greater powers than you can imagine. You have an infinite source of power, intelligence, and wealth within you that you can use to change your circumstances in life. Your distorted belief of powerlessness has produced all the unfavorable circumstances and sufferings in your life. Learn the truth about your power and create a happy life and favorable circumstances.

Remind yourself that you are in control of your life and world. What comes planned or unplanned should not determine how you feel; you should choose how you feel. This control means you control what is truly yours, which are your feelings, reactions, and emotions.

What happens externally is not your business, so do not frustrate yourself trying to control it.

When you are in control of what is truly yours, events and people will not determine what kind of day you should have. Nothing that happens outside will affect your mood or feelings. If you are letting people or events ruin your peace or happiness, it means you are giving them the control of your life or day. You should not let the ignorance or weakness of others determine your day or life.

When you assume the victim attitude and identify yourself as a victim of a person, circumstances, and institutions, these things will look like overpowering, giant problems that dominate and overwhelm all the aspects of your life. Even the most harmless person will look to you like a powerful, dominant, cruel, and evil tyrant who has made you powerless and hopeless. You exaggerate the influence of that person or circumstance in your life. You believe that, because of that person or situation, your life has been destroyed. Who can destroy your life? Why do you give that much power to another human over your life? How can you become so fearful and cowardly? Which life are you afraid to lose? The fearful and cowardly life? If you consciously face your fears, it is not your life that you will lose but the illusions that have robbed you of life. The illusion of living as a victim and a coward will be gone. You will realize that the people who you thought are victimizing you are the most powerless and fearful.

Seeking Pain and Hurt

Some people are overwhelmed by the pain and sufferings they created for themselves through their wretched perceptions. To a wretched man, these are among the things that are also wretched to him: his life, the weather, his city, his family, his marriage, his divorce, his friends, his voice, his birthplace, his job, his boss, his career, his past, his future, his present, his name, his body, his health, his emotions, his confidence, his courage, his wealth, his poverty, his education, his skills, his talents, his style, his colleagues, his neighbors. Everything and everyone he comes close to is wretched, because he sees the world through the glass of wretchedness. He has the ability to turn everything into bad and will always find something to complain about. Nothing will change for him until he changes the perception through which he is looking at the world.

To a wretched man, even those things he succeeded in, he will look at them as failures and misfortunes. His perspectives become so crooked that he looks at all his life and sees nothing but wretchedness and failure.

Likewise, the sad man, if he is not saddened by other people or circumstances, will go on to search for sad music, other sad people, sad documentaries, sad movies, and other things to feel sad. It is his ego that is trying to change the present into a sad moment. Even in your most boring time, do not fall for this trick of the ego that burdens you with more sadness. Instead, you can look for something fun to do, some other activities you enjoy.

The ego looks for chances to get angry, hurt, or disrespected. The ego is sometimes in an imaginary fight with other people. The ego doesn't want peace and looks for cheap and flimsy excuses to get angry. It majors the minor issues. At the end, the ego is wasting your energy, time, and peace of mind by actively seeking these imaginary fights. The person who loses at the end is you. This is a war on self that rarely bothers others, as these conflicts take place mostly in your mind. I have never had an enemy outside myself. The ego is the main enemy; recognition and observation are the only weapons that destroy it.

11

What Is Not Life

Modern Exploitation

One of the worst exploitations of our modern life is the lack of moderation regarding how much time we spend on different forms of media. This is done through news, reality and drama TV episodes, documentaries, social media like Facebook and Twitter, sports channels, and so on. Those are things that waste your precious time that you could have used to learn more about yourself and connect with the infinite intelligence within you. Your time is as important as Donald Trump's time or news about him. Your life is as important to you as his life is important to him. So why should you waste your life watching other people's lives?

Wasting many hours of your day watching others' lives or news is wanton negligence of your own life and the infinite intelligence within. Why should you waste your precious and limited time on this earth watching the life or news on Donald Trump or any other person? The most important news is what is happening in your life, in your own world.

I watched on TV people, including children, impersonating Elvis. That is worshipping of an idol, which undermines your self-worth as you value more the looks and lifestyle of another human being.

You are as much a star as Elvis. All this worshipping of the idols, royals, and celebrities will disintegrate your wholeness and take away the power from you since it means you acknowledge that there is another soul more important than you. Worship and adore the one in you. Admire and celebrate your own life and gifts. I worship no masters, no royals, no writers, and no history. Will you have the time to notice and celebrate the good things in your life if you pay all your attention to celebrating other people's lives?

Becoming Enslaved by the System

The modern economic system and media has systematically enslaved the majority of the world population. This enslavement takes place in form of debts like mortgage, credit card debt, car debt, and student loans. It is also through addiction and dependence on TV, the internet, social media, experts, music, movies, education, and others. These things are not harmful in moderation, but if they consume a significant part of your life, then you have enslaved yourself. The excessive consumption or heavy dependence on any of this has killed the creativity of the masses and made them powerless intellectually, financially, and spiritually. It has also contributed to the growth of the wealth gap between the haves and have-nots, as the majority of us have become heavily dependent on a few institutions and people from whom we consume. You are not only paying your money to get these materials, but you are paying with your life. All the products, entertainment, experts, spiritual teachers, TV programs, movies, music, sports, social media, internet trends, and other pleasures want a piece of you, a piece of your precious time. Money is not even a big concern here; the problem is wasting power, interest, attention, belief, energy, and time on them.

The other life-wasting endeavor is the focus given to the end rather than the means, hence wasting your energy and time thinking about and seeking fame and fortune. There is a culture of too much consumerism of materials, idol worshiping, worshiping of your boss, with addiction to education, TV, the internet, social media, watching sports, and music and movies. Following celebrities and leaders on Twitter, the cult-like following of experts like chefs to learn cooking, spiritual leaders to get enlightened or saved, stock analysts to get rich, physical exercise gurus to get more fit, yoga masters, and other perceived role models.

All these activities have withdrawn the force from individuals and severely hampered their creativity. The haves control the majority of the population through provision of consumer goods, social media platforms, style, cultural dominance, expert knowledge, financial means, entertainment, and spiritual teachings. The power is concentrated among the few who control these aspects of our lives. The majority of us have stopped producing and have become helpless consumers and helplessly in financial debt for a lifetime. So how do you expect to change your situation if you only consume and never produce?

No one, including spiritual leaders, should create cult-like followers and lifetime dependents. Even kids leave their parents' house at some point and start their own lives. Your job as a spiritual leader should be to encourage and enable independence rather than creating lifetime dependence. Your job as a spiritual leader is to guide others to achieve personal liberation but not bondage. There is no bondage that is good, not even a spiritual one. The good ceases to be good when it enslaves you.

There is a rise in financial conmen who pose as spiritual leaders. These imposters have lifetime followers or members who regularly pay for materials that perpetuate their dependence on the spiritual leader. The leaders create a feeling of "you are not good enough" among their followers, who have to read one more book, attend one more seminar, and even buy an app to become complete or enlightened or happier. It is like a school with no end or graduation; you become their student for the rest of your life.

The focus of the spiritual leaders should be to remind people of the treasures and the power they have within. Instead of empowering their followers, most spiritual leaders make their followers feel incomplete, powerless, and insecure.

What is the use of enlightenment if you end up wasting many or all the years of your life trying to get enlightened? Why waste all your precious years trying to get enlightened or preparing for what happens to you after death? Does the afterlife matter if you never lived in the first place? You cannot live on this earth for eternity; you have limited years. Why do you spend those years learning how to live rather than enjoying your life? Do mammals or babies practice to suckle the tits of their mothers for hours? If they spend a lot of time practicing before they start suckling, they will die of hunger; instead, they start suckling immediately, and they become better at it with time. That is the same in life. You have very few years to live. Do not die before truly living them. Suckle the tits of life as soon as possible. Don't waste your entire life analyzing how to suckle.

You can read a book that teaches you how to swim for a whole year, but you will never truly learn how to swim until you get into the water and start practicing the movements. Also, you can learn about life only through experience. Let your life unfold naturally and learn from your daily experience and interactions.

You can spend all your life listening to others and quoting and reading others' books and teachings, but they will have no use if you do not apply them and relate them to your daily life. The greatest books ever written and the greatest masters all point you to the truth that is within you. Hence, you should be paying great attention to yourself. You do not have the luxury of spending this life as a rehearsal to live another life better. So many great minds have wasted their lives without contributing to this world because they always looked to be in preparation to live. Live each day with the awareness that it could be your last. You should go about life the way you know how to and the only way you can experience it, and that is your way.

Live a life of courage, supreme confidence, happiness, peace, fearlessness, and abundance. A life of fully accepting and appreciating your portion. Love your life as it is and as if it cannot be more perfect.

Substance Abuse and the Vicious Cycle

There is a proverb in Amharic language that says "Wuha Kida, Wuha Melis." It means scooping and pouring back the water into the same container again and again. There is nothing you are doing if all day you scoop and pour back the water. Sometimes, that is all we do unconsciously, all day and all year, doing and undoing the same thing. Making a mistake that you have made many times before and spending your days and years trying to correct that same mistake or habit. You waste your time and energy repeating the same habits and then spend more time and energy trying to overcome or correct them. Even with all the knowledge of the negative impacts of the bad habits, you keep coming back to them. Look back at all the days or years these habits have wasted away and imagine how different your life would have been if not for the habits. Look at how the habit negatively impacted your life and the lives of your loved ones.

Let's look at smoking. After you start smoking, you will then waste a lot of energy and time trying to stop smoking and analyzing the problem. The truth for many is they have gone through the same process, action, and reaction many times before. You do that all over again, wasting years or the whole of your life before you know it. It is a vicious cycle that slowly consumes the whole of your life. You spend all your life committing the same few mistakes and the same process of correcting them over and over. This is the definition of insanity. These are the kinds of mistakes you should focus on overcoming at the beginning, because they are wasting a significant part of your life and energy.

It is much better to commit new mistakes and learn new things from the new mistakes than getting stuck on one. Identify the bad habits that have become a life-wasting vicious cycle, and each time you are tempted to repeat them, remind yourself of all the pain and suffering they have caused. Imagine the happier and healthier days you will have ahead. Do not focus on the pain and effects of withdrawal.

Remember, you have the strength and power of the infinite intelligence within you. The substances have no power over you.

Puffing the Smoke

Today I felt unease, so I smoked cigarettes for ease.
Yesterday it was the weather, so I smoked to whither.
Oh, the day before yesterday, that was the stress, so I smoked to feel less intense.
Today it is happy hour, so with friends I smoked another.

There is an endless hole in my soul
That I will never be able to fill
With sex, smoke, or a pill.
The more I take, the more I crave,
Until an overdose sends me to my early grave.

Every time, it starts with the promise that this is last,
A promise the endless hole breaks with another lust.

Smoking or Doing Drugs over Anger, Stress, or Challenge

A fool's life is full of worry about life, the same life they cared so much about. They worry and get sick and smoke or abuse drugs to cover those feelings. Therefore, they shorten that same life they cared so much about through self-harming actions and emotions and then end up dead without really living.

What are the things that are making you not live your life? Shortening your life?

How can you chase away the same thing you are searching for?

Why lose life searching for life? Abusing drugs, smoking and excessive drinking are the most cowardly ways of responding to challenges in life. Instead of facing the challenge head-on, like a courageous person, you instead cower and resort to hurting your body. It means you are taking out your anger and frustration on the most innocent, which in this case is your body. Why not face the causes and triggers of those angers and frustration head-on? That is what courage is. It is not cowering into your dark corner and hurting your body by lightning up a cigarette or abusing other drugs or alcohol.

What you do in private when you are alone matters a lot. It reveals your true strength of character and how you handle situations. You either cower in your dark corner and start hurting yourself by smoking, drinking, doing drugs, or other harmful things or you step out of your dark corner and fight back with courage and determination.

Are you transmuting the challenges for your benefit and strength or you have become the slave of the challenges, and hence you are destroying yourself and wasting your life in hurt and misery? Do not exacerbate your challenges by abusing drugs. They bring more serious and permanent problems. Look at what is challenging you, and you will realize that it is not worth taking away your health. If you have a financial or relationship problem and you start abusing drugs to numb your pain, the problems will not go away; instead, they get worse. The drug abuse or drinking will shift your attention from finding a solution to creating more problems. You will end up dealing with new self-inflicted problems of drug abuse while the original problem remains unsolved or gets worse. You cannot solve financial issues by spending money on drugs, and you cannot solve relationship problems by abusing drugs, as it will worsen your relationship with friends and loved ones.

Modern Medicine

If you are consistently taking modern medicine to take care of ailments like ulcers, blood pressure, diabetes, uric acid, or any other diseases that are caused by your lifestyle, you are harming the temple of God more than curing yourself. You are treating the symptoms rather than the causes. You are being a fool, eating toxins and poisons that are harming the temple of God and trying to get relief from the simple and necessary pains that are there to send you a message to stop you from the self-harm. It's like you keep burning your hands by putting them over a hot stove, and instead of stopping this self-harm, you are focused on what kind of cream or painkillers you should take to stop or reduce the pain from the burn. Stop self-inflicted pain and harming the temple of God and start living a healthy life. Listen to your body and stop whatever is harming it.

12

True Living

The City and the Star

I was on the twenty-sixth floor of Calgary city tower,
Observing a dark sky that deemed the stars' power.
The city was asleep except for cab drivers and partygoers.
From the top and afar, the city looks like a big Christmas tree.
I am one of the lights in this tree and one soul.
I give out my light that makes up part of the whole.
I was calmly enjoying my strange thoughts.
The sky was dark. I saw only one star.
She must be feeling lonely,
Or maybe she has the company
Of other stars that I cannot see.
And she must be laughing at my thoughts.
I was waiting for the star to tell me her story
And waiting for the city to tell me her story.

The city says to me, "In my stomach, I carry the world."
"What world?" I asked her. To which she replied,
"I carry happiness and sadness, life and death,
Victory and defeat, love and hate."
Then I asked the city, "Why do you carry both?

I mean, the negative and the positive emotions.
Why not carry only the positive?" To which she answered,
"I carry both because they are equally important.
Both are just as beautiful." But I protested in disagreement,
"How dare you say that to me? Both are not the same."
She then replied calmly with an air of a sage's wisdom,
"Both are the same to me. It's the way you look at them.
They are both sent to enrich you, if you gladly welcome them."

A little disappointed by her simple explanation.
A lifetime I spent to answer this question.
I wanted to walk away from the conversation.
Controlling my anger, I asked her why she wasted all this time
To reveal her secrets and explain the duality of life.
She said to me, "All things happen at the perfect moment."
She added, "You look at it as a waste, and I look at it as perfect.
It cannot be more perfect."
Then I said to her in surrender, "You have a big stomach to carry all."
Then she reminded me, "You have bigger; emotions need not a
physical store."

Next, I moved on to listen to the story of the star.
I wanted to take her picture before she disappeared into the sky.
I was worried she would leave me without saying goodbye.
Shame on me; my phone camera cannot get a clear picture of her.
Or is she playing hard to get, and to her beauty, I concur.
I blurted out, "I know you! I have seen you before!"
She answered me with swagger, "I know you too."
She said, "I have observed you from the day you were born,
Before you came to this world, and I will be there after you are gone."

I was too scared to ask her what happens to me after I leave.
Does she even know? I didn't know what to believe.
I will keep that question for another day,
I said to myself, not wanting to know the reply.

"So, what have you seen me do?" I was so curious.
She said, "Everything in your life comes and goes."
She then wondered, "Why do you waste your short time in this world
On fear, pain, hate, revenge, regrets, hurts, and sadness?
They are all created by your worldview and the way you judge.

"You can create the high energies of life like happiness,
Good health, courage, abundance, love, and success."
She reiterated that my perspective matters.
"Change your worldviews to see the miracles.
Do not focus on the weaknesses of others
Or dim your light and depend on their opinions.

"Do not dim your light admiring the light of other stars.
Shine when it pains, shine when it rains.
Shine in happiness and shine in sadness
Shine always, shine regardless."
Those were her last words.
I felt both the city and the star conspired
To teach me the same lesson on this night.
I walked away wondering if these two communicate
And share our secrets when we all sleep.

Components of Success and Failure

A lot of people are fooled by the ego into thinking that they are their job and career or title and therefore expect to be respected and respect themselves, depending on those false identities. The value of your life doesn't depend on your title, career, level of wealth, or background. You are as important as anybody in this world. No one will leave this life with these titles, positions, or riches. The mistake people make is that they value themselves or have low self-esteem due to their current social status, such that they get incapable of achieving anything better in life. How can the world respect you if you don't respect yourself?

These people wrongly expect wealth or titles to give them respectable status or dignity or self-esteem. If you get an Olympic gold medal for a hundred-meter, but you never ran, never exercised, and never competed, will the honorary receipt of the gold medal make you an athlete or a possible winner of the next Olympics or other athletic competitions? No. It will add nothing to your odds of winning, and the medal cannot make you an athlete. What makes a champion is not the medal but the process of mental and physical training, competing, and winning. The gold is a symbol of these processes. I call these processes components of success. You cannot say you will start exercising, competing, and getting the right mental attitude only after getting the medal.

Nothing works like that, not in this world. That is not how life or nature work. Similarly, stop thinking that you will have the components of success, such as self-respect, courage, integrity, self-confidence, happiness, peace, good health, and the positive mental attitude, only after accomplishing great things in life or after becoming successful in life. No athlete would say, "I will train after I become a champion." Instead, you train to become a champion. As well, self-respect, courage, integrity, self-confidence, happiness, peace, good health, and a positive mental attitude are components of success that make up the symbols of success, such as great accomplishments or a successful life. They will come naturally and inevitably when you put those components together throughout your life, not at the end.

A lot of people try to reverse this flow of nature and hence remain stuck or achieve nothing in life or fail to reach their goals. This is because they are focused on the symbols rather than the components of success.

The river can never carry the log upstream. The log floats downstream naturally. Travel with the current of nature by understanding its flow. This will help you not to miss out on life as you enjoy the journey.

Your great achievements will look so easy and natural to others because you understood what is important.

Below are some of these components of success:

- courage
- fearlessness
- confidence
- spiritual harmony
- good health
- physical exercise
- eating healthy
- happiness
- peace of mind
- great self-esteem
- great self-respect
- self-love
- loving others
- acceptance and contentment
- faith and belief and trust
- kindness
- persistence and grit
- forgiveness
- valuing your time
- great self-expression or communication skills
- meditation
- positive attitude

Below are also some components of failure:

- fear
- shame
- guilt
- complaining
- confusion
- pain
- worry
- stress
- anger
- hate
- revenge
- discomfort
- sadness
- superiority complex
- inferiority complex
- victimhood
- attachment to past or the future
- material attachments
- sense of incompleteness
- neediness
- anxiety
- self-doubt
- wasting your time or boredom

The Illusion of Roles

I sometimes wonder about the illusion we have created around ourselves by valuing each human according to their roles and status in society. We easily forget that these are categories that we created, and they are all illusions of who we think we are. We spend the rest of our lives defending these illusions.

The reality is that we are all the same, human beings. We are greater than any role in this world. We should talk to, respect, and treat everyone in the same way. We should value everyone as a human first, regardless of their roles. This practice will not only benefit the other person but also ourselves. It will replace the fears, suspicions, and discriminations we have for each other based on roles and replace those feelings with mutual love, respect, and understanding.

Changing Faces

The changing of faces here means waiting for that day when all things get better for you to start living courageously and with respect. Life never comes around twice; you can never get back this time or moment. Live life. Live courageously. Courage is the only means through which your life will get better. Choosing to abandon the components of success to get by or to move to better days is a waste of life because those better days will never come as long as you don't understand the flow and current of life. Your dreams are not dreams but nightmares if they require you to compromise or abandon the components of success. Any day could be your last. Do not live a miserable life now for a better tomorrow.

Otherwise, life will treat you like a dirt because you covered your internal treasures with dirt by abandoning the components of success. Cheaply giving away your courage, dignity, and confidence for an illusion of job security, friendship, or other little favors will result in a miserable life. The best day to get courage and to live supremely is now.

If you lose your courage and integrity so as to get love from other people or because you hope to gain financially, for job security, or to look good to others or maintain a relationship, then you deserve none of those things. You deserve nothing good in life if you live fearfully and shortchange your integrity for the sake of material gain. Living in fear will lead to a loss of everything in life. If you continue living in a bad marriage because you fear losing the love of your kids, then you deserve neither their love nor a good life.

If you continue working in a place where you work fearfully and get mistreated, but you don't quit because you hope to get a promotion or you fear to lose income, then you deserve none of the good things at work or respect. You will be probably the first person to be fired from that job and the last person to get any raise or promotions. The most precious thing to lose in your life is your integrity. Once you live in fear or give away your integrity, there is only one outcome, and that is a miserable life.

If you are waiting to be treated with respect or plan to respect yourself when you get that good job or wealth, then you will die before receiving any respect in life. You are divine, respectable, important, and lovable now in this very state and circumstance. Do not attach your dignity to something external. You are a complete human now; do not hope for anything external to complete you. If you have someone in your life that does not respect you now because you don't have a good job or you are not wealthy now, do not try to impress them or gain their respect by seeking material wealth. People who value others based on material wealth or any other external thing have very little respect for themselves. Try not to spend too much time with people who disrespect you now because they think you are less of a human based on your wealth, status, or occupation.

There are a lot of people who are wasting their lives because they seek respect and dignity in something external. They live unfulfilled lives because they believe the job they are doing now or the amount of wealth they have now is not good enough to afford them a respectable life. As a result, they feel small and less human. They do not respect themselves or expect respect from others in their current situation or job. They wait for that illusory day when they will get rich or get a good job so that they can demand respect from others and respect themselves.

Some people get stuck on one of these false identities or faces, even though they earlier planned that this was just one of the identities they were adopting to get by or reach that ultimate goal when they would feel fulfilled, respected, and worthy or important. So, some people get stuck on these early identities where they feel unworthy or unfulfilled, and eventually this state of mind becomes the biggest obstacle to achieving their desired goals, and they will probably die before seeing that great or beautiful future.

Respect the One with Whom You Live Forever

Respect the one with whom you live forever, and that is you. Everyone comes and goes in your life, and the majority of them stay with you for a very short time. And no one stays with you for every second of your life until the day you take your last breath, except you. You have to give this person the greatest of love, respect, appreciation, forgiveness, loyalty, happiness, good health, peace, and courage.

If there is anybody that you should idolize in this world, it is you. All the wonders and powers of the world are in you. All the beauties and arts of the world are in you. All the wisdom and intelligence of the world are in you. All the poems and essays of the world are in you.

Treat yourself like royalty. Be gentle and loving to yourself. All the good things you do for yourself are the good you do for the world. You give what you have; you give good if and only you have good.

What You Own Owns You

For many, what they own enslaves them. They live a life of worry, fear, anxiety, perturbation, and confusion because they fear losing what they have. They feel compelled to act and live in a certain way to portray their status, hence not living according to nature or according to their nature. They are not free people. They have willingly become slaves of their material possessions.

Never Leave Your Dhabbinn

Never leave your dhabbinn; never leave your eternal treasures.
Never leave supreme confidence, courage, or abundance.
Never leave your peace of mind, spiritual harmony, or happiness.

Never leave your dhabbinn, not for anyone or anything in this world.
Not for a career; if you leave, you become a slave.
Not for money; if you leave, you will be penniless.
Not for gods; if you leave, you will be godless.
Not for heaven; if you leave, you will be in hell.
Not for peace; if you leave, you will be in chaos.
Leaving your dhabbinn is idolatry.

Come back to your dhabbinn to reclaim your kingdom,
To anchor your principles and make you whole
And offer you guidance in this treacherous world.
No good in gaining the world by forfeiting your soul.

The Most Important Is You

You already own the most important things in the world, the most precious things. All the wealth in the world cannot come close to those things that you have within. It is the lack of knowledge and the realization of these treasures that makes you feel poor and needy. When you give away these treasures, which I call dhabbinn, for anything in the world, then you lose everything, including the things you thought you gained in exchange for these internal treasures. Keep them and protect them with your life as the most important treasures in your life. Be loyal to them and enjoy them; they are the source of eternal happiness and joy. Know that you already have them and nobody can take them away or give them to you. We all have them; some recognize them, and some don't, and that is all the difference.

These treasures (your dhabbinn) are your dignity, confidence, courage, self-respect, health, spirituality, peace of mind, contentment, independence, love, forgiveness, and happiness etc., they are your treasures within. You have these; you have all the treasures of the world. (Dhabbinn is a word from Oromo language that closely means your principles).

Success is not what you gain but what you give, and the first and true success is never leaving your dhabbinn. Instead, offer hard work, a positive attitude, encouragement, and love to make the lives of others better, and it will all come back to you in abundance.

13

The Illusion of Loss

One with Nothing to Lose Fears Loss Most

People with few possessions or at the bottom of a career ladder have the greatest fear of losing the little they have. Fear made them not try new things or dream big; hence their life condition remains the same or gets worse with time. The illusion of scarcity fills them with the fear of losing the little they have. The constant thoughts of scarcity make them fear the future. They think it cannot get better but worse. So, is it a surprise if they live the life they imagined? They will reap what they sow. They live in conditions of poverty and scarcity created by their own imagination. The power of their subconscious mind brought into reality the dominant thoughts of their conscious mind. They had the power to bring poverty and scarcity into their lives, and they have as much power to bring wealth and abundance into their lives. These people with illusions of scarcity are resigned to a false fact that success and the good life are for a few chosen. They blame their poor life's condition on their past, birthplace, family, political condition, economic condition, and other external factors. This blame keeps them from examining their dominant thoughts, beliefs, or responsibilities that contributed to their condition. The finger-pointing and the search for answers outside of themselves makes them powerless to do anything that improves their life's condition. They desperately cling to the meager earning or career and eventually lose the little they have, due to their fear and intense neediness. The preoccupation with their little fortune limits their time and energy to explore better opportunities or careers.

On your deathbed is when all things lose their significance, and you will come to regret the wasting of your life on fear and desperation. You spend your life in fear, worry, desperation, and other forms of negative energy just to live or protect what you have or prolong your years on this earth. Have you really lived if that is how you spent your life? What does a good life mean to you? Do not waste a single day on life-wasting energies. Enjoy each day of your life and empower yourself with positive thoughts. If one farmer tells you that he has ten cows, including six that just died, and another farmer tells you he has eight cows, including two that just died, which of the two farmers has more cows? Off course, it is the second farmer with six cows that are alive. Many people believe a good life means a long life because they include the dead years in their lives, just like the two farmers. The years you spent on life-wasting energies are your dead years, so don't focus on the number of years you live but how well you live each day.

WEALTH DISPARITY

I read on news that the 9 richest people on earth have more wealth than half of the in this world or more than 4 billion people. So, what makes some few so rich and the majority poor? Why the little man who has no steak in the horse race has more fear, worry, anxiety and other negative emotions about the horse race. Why the man with so little has so much fear of loss? What does he have to lose, which wealth? Why does he have so much frustrations and stress about losing/protecting his wealth, career and job or savings. What job are you afraid to lose, the job that is paying you peanuts? Why clinging so much to poverty and mediocrity? You see, the poor man is focused and concerned about what he can get from others. He thinks in terms of taking but not giving, he thinks in terms of dependence. He thinks in terms of scarcity but not abundance. When he thinks about his job, career or employment, he is thinking about what he can get from them i.e. salary, job, security, insurance, retirement benefits, promotion etc. not what he can give his employers, society, country or the world. The takers hand is always scarce and dependent. This selfish thought of dependence on others, kills his creativity, abundance and independence. He lives with fear of losing the small income or favors he gets from his employers. He thinks he is incapable of producing or giving. For him a good year or time means, he kept his job but not producing something new or trying to be a creator, security of his mediocre life is his main concern. He fears independent thoughts or creating new things or ideas. He does not believe in creation, whether invisible or visible. He lives cowardly and with strict discipline in the world given to him and thus walks carefully between the lines, afraid to express his unique talents and ideas, he does not think of changing the world, as he has no time, gut or free will. For him astronomical success, infinite intelligence and abundance are illusions, the reality for him is scarcity, limitations and sufferings. He worships the past tradition, beliefs, and ideas of his ancestors or community even though, they are all living in poverty and mediocrity for generations. He thinks to himself, "who is he to change the old rules?" so he becomes their slave, thus he never believes in becoming the master of his destiny or fate. The illusions of lose makes him desperately cling to the little he has. For him all his time, efforts, education and energy are targeted towards becoming the best employee or the best dependant on others, so this shapes his ideas, actions and behaviors. So, this man is already poor in thoughts (invisible creations), how can he be rich in life (visible world). His life is monotonous, archaic, mechanical and predictable and not interesting or thrilling. Therefore, he tries to find thrills and interest by dedicating his time and attention, watching, judging, analyzing and admiring other people's life on news or social media. He sees nothing interesting about his life, that is why he has secure and predictable life, he knows when to retire, with what amount of saving, insurance policy etc. that makes him happy and secure. His employer, financial advisor and insurance agent had already forecasted, predicated and predetermined his life, so he lives accordingly. Therefore, no more motivations for invisible creations, living in faith or trying to create new things or ideas. So how can he get anywhere in life? Is this interesting life?

I am giving you the map, you walk, ride or drive there, it is your choice not to make even any move. The choice is yours my friend. You need courage and an open mind to learn and gain the wisdom/ enlightenment/right-mindedness, if you think your cup of exploring and learning new wisdoms is full, what can I do for you? You are already full and a fool.

You Are Not Fair to Your Employer

When you live in fear of losing your job, you are not being fair to yourself or your employer. Your fear leads to bad performance at work, negative emotions and a negative environment at work, and a feeling of grudge and hate and suspicion toward your employer and colleagues at work. You poison the workplace environment, and so it is only fair that you get fired. These fears and anxiety are also going to negatively affect your relationships with your family and friends.

Now, you see how you created all these problems through your thoughts of fear and anxiety, and you end up blaming and hating other people for all these outcomes. Instead, get rid of these illusions and empower yourself.

Ninety-Two Years Census Question

On the Canadian census form, there is a question about consent to allow the Canadian government to use your information for research purposes after ninety-two years. At that time, literally no one I know or see on the street or in the market or on the news will be alive. Not the rich, the famous, the poor, the victim, the brave, the talented, poet, writer, inventor, or president will live to see that day. We will be all gone as a generation. I will be gone definitely long before that. Then you look at life and ask yourself why a lot of people are so stressed about life after all, holding too tightly to this vanity.

From Those Who Have Little

In one of his parables in the Bible (Mathew 25:14–30), Jesus talks about three servants who were entrusted with money by their master. The first two were given five and two bags of silver, and they doubled the money given to them through investment. The third, who was given only a bag of silver, buried the money because he was afraid to lose it. To those who think of abundance and leverage whatever money, talent, education, skills, love, courage, and confidence they have, they will be entrusted with more, and they will have more blessings. To those who dwell on scarcity, fear, and blame, then the little they have will be taken away from them by their own thoughts and beliefs, and they will have a life of misery, pain, fear, scarcity, and many other problems.

If you don't think of your talents as abundant and leverage them to achieve greater things, then those talents will be taken away from you as you failed to recognize, enhance, or use them. You have to recognize and trust the infinite intelligence and abundance within you and appreciate what you have. All your problems are created by the egoistic mind that veiled the infinite intelligence within and overwhelmed you with thoughts of fear, scarcity, and lack. Come back to yourself, and you will find everything there. Do not search for solutions outside. That is the ego's habit of making you feel powerless and inadequate. Within you lies the greatest treasures and talents on earth. Learn to recognize, value, appreciate, and enhance them to enjoy a life of abundance.

The people who have great wealth and homes and other properties put their seed or little money in the right vehicle of growth or investment, and it grew and multiplied. If you are investing your seed or small money in the wrong place or spend unwisely, your sufferings, problems, poverty, pain, diseases, and perturbation will grow, not your wealth. It is a straightforward and simple rule. You harvest what you sow in life. It is not a miracle.

It is not how much you get but how and where you spend your money that matters. Are you spending your money as a seed to bring you more wealth, peace, prosperity, health, happiness, and other good things in life, or you are spending your money as a seed to bring you diseases, lack of peace, drugs, and many other problems? If you cannot be trusted with the small, how can you be trusted with bigger wealth?

It is one small seed that becomes the giant tree or the many grains or fruits that the farmer harvests. It is the small and simple knowledge, skill, and gifts that become astronomical successes and infinite abundance and blessings. Understand nature and you will get all the answers to life.

Plant the small seed, the small gift, skill, wealth, and blessings, and they will grow infinitely and abundantly and astronomically. Understand the flow of nature, and you will have all the wisdom of life.

The majority of people fail in life because they are frustrated with not having big success or want to start with big success or focus on the big success or why they don't have it. This misunderstanding ends up wasting their time and energy. The wise grow small skills, wealth, and gifts to achieve astronomical success, knowing that all things start small. They look at all the astronomical successes and blessings of others and know they all started small. They do not say, "Why I do not have big successes and blessings like that?" They know small is big, if you plant it and value it.

How can a farmer keep the few grains in his hands and never plant them and instead complain and focus on why he does not have as many seeds as his next-door farmer who planted the few seeds and filled his store or silo with the harvest? Don't hold your seeds in your hands or waste your time wondering at the success of your neighbor. Plant your few seeds and fill up your store.

Your few seeds can be the money you have, your writing skills, financial skills, leadership skills, athletic skills, public speaking skills, political leadership skills, spiritual leadership skills, computer skills, or any other skills in life. Plant it and harvest the astronomical success and blessings. Don't die with those few skills or gifts in your hands. They have infinite potential to make the world a better place. It was the infant yesterday who changed the world today.

Look for the small advantages in your life and leverage them to achieve greater things and be grateful. It is the tiniest single cell that make up the complex human being that has a complex brain and does complex things. Nature thrives in simplicity. Nature is simple and beautiful. Similarly, it is the small knowledge or skill that you have that will build astronomical things or success.

14

Anger

Boxing Yourself

Most people box their life and experience
Around a few people they know and see,
Making their perspective so small in that case,
Seeing this world with the smallest lens.

I watched on TV about young people protecting their turf,
Killing each other and acting so rough.
Then I thought to myself, *I do just the same.*
Though I don't kill and maim,
I very much frustrate and stress over my claim.

We all do this irrational behavior,
Limiting our thoughts and actions
To what we see every day and lose our imaginations
Of the bigger world and alternatives.

Instead we are determined to alienate
This brother, this sister who lives next door.
Killing or hating them is not the solution,
For we cannot hate or kill them all

To have peace and live by ourselves alone.

What about love? What about a move?
But be careful, brother.
If you move to a new place with the old heart,
It won't be long before someone gets hurt.
But with love, with love, you don't need to move,
And if you move, you move to more love.

Imagine a place where you live with peace and love.
Make that place in your heart.
You will soon realize
All places are like that.

Anger and Rage

I had many thoughts of getting into a fight with people in the past. It sounds crazy, I know, me thinking of hurting somebody after all this enlightenment and education and wisdom. But yes, like all the other people who are already in prison, I was overcome by rage and hate sometimes. That confirms my belief of not judging those killers and other criminals who committed heinous crimes in a moment of insane rage and hate that ended up with someone seriously getting hurt or killed. I had that moment even though I did not follow up with the action, which was the next natural thing to do.

The only little difference between me and those murderers in jail is that I sometimes reflect on my thoughts and remind myself that this is the egoistic mind, this is not the real me. This was around the time I was going through spiritual transformation and self-discovery. I was otherwise a well-behaved, nice guy, but I had those moments of anger. I truly empathize with those brothers and sisters who are in jail for murder and other crimes. My experience gave me a window of opportunity to understand how the egoistic mind possessed their thoughts for a short time and led them to commit those crimes.

Next time the same thoughts come to me, I would want to just observe how I am handling it and write them down immediately. The other major lesson I learned was that when I started working out at the gym, those bad thoughts disappeared, especially when I was listening to music and working out.

I really advise others to do the same to cool off their anger. Step away from the situation for a little bit and calm yourself by engaging in activities that will take your mind away from the anger. The thoughts of hurting someone will hurt you more than the other person. There is no way you can hurt another without hurting yourself.

Sometimes we are angry and frustrated because of the lack or inability to express ourselves. The people who cannot express their true feelings freely are the ones who are most angry and frustrated. They cannot express their true feelings, so they are filled with anger inside. You should get disagreements off your chest immediately and clearly to have more peace, and the other person will have more peace too because they will know where you stand and will try to make amends.

The inferior ego seethes and fumes with anger in silence. This ego will waste life by replaying past conflicts or disagreements. In its replay, the ego assumes the position of a winner and argues and fights the illusory enemy. This inferior ego will have an imagined conversation with the perceived enemy and gets angry as if the fight or argument is actually taking place now.

This illusion will lead to disturbed mind and peace, a waste of energy through anger, and a waste of time on illusions. It steals away joy and happiness, reduces productivity, disrupts creative thinking, steals away your time from beautiful imaginations, veils you from God (infinite intelligence within) and may also lead to a possible real confrontation with the perceived enemy in case you meet him/her.

Of course, as is the case with all forms of illusions, the best action to stop this is by observing your thoughts and remembering that it is just in the nature of the mind to wander. Look at it as a lie of the little, inferior ego. Don't waste your time trying to fight it and don't believe any of its lies about the imaginary enemy. There is no enemy in reality but just people seeking your love and attention. Live with peace and love with everyone. Love your brothers and sisters. Don't let their weakness make you weak. Forgive them, for they don't know what they are doing or saying most of the time.

Answer any question in any disagreement on the spot and never replay it in your mind afterward. The inferior ego looks at harmless questions as confrontation with others, since it does not have the courage to face others and express its concerns. The confrontation takes place when you are alone and can grow into a rage.

Be courageous and fearless and solve the conflict right there and then. Don't walk away or smile when challenged. Give your opinions and answers immediately. Be true to yourself and the other person. Do not fear arguments or conflicts and do not try to hold back because you want to save the relationship. You will get better relationships if you have open communication, and the relationship with the other person will improve.

Do not let the ego lie to you that the illusions of the fights in your hallucinations are proof of courage and fearlessness. These hallucinations and illusions are proof of inferiority and cowardice in reality. The only person you are fighting and wasting away is you. Probably, nobody is even aware of your hallucinations or the rage going on within your mind. The ego tries to convince you that these hallucinations are real. Once you start observing the ego at play, do not worry if they come back again and again, because this is the nature of the mind, and it will take some time before the habit completely goes away. But the moment you create this awareness, you are cured. The subsequent hallucinations are harmless and useless, as you are now able to recognize them and see them for what they are.

Anger and Hurt

The thoughts of people hurting you or making you a victim are based on illusions that gave the other person power over you. You can only get hurt when you choose to focus on the actions or weaknesses of others and you put yourself in a victim position. The hurt comes as a result of expecting good acts from all people all the time. We get hurt by another person's weak judgment, but we should remember that the person is living in their own world, acting as they should, according to their thoughts and worldview. It is difficult to understand other people's thought systems or perspectives that motivated them to take certain actions, but all selfish acts of hurting other people are as a result of ignorance and a distorted worldview.

Nothing in this world can hurt you if you don't let it. You are the creator of your world; you decide whether to create a world of joy, victory, peace, and courage or a world of victimhood, fear, and hurt. You decide to see what you want to see, feel how you want to feel, and act how you want to act or respond.

I have witnessed the devastating effects of holding grudges and vengeful thoughts. I have seen them destroy individual lives and lives of millions as a group. You should not become a hostage of another person's weaknesses. Do not wait for them to apologize or compensate their past wrongdoing by becoming good to you. If they are good, it is mostly for themselves, and if they are bad, it is in the same measure bad for themselves. Become good to yourself and for yourself, and then you can share the good with others.

Holding grudges or thoughts of vengeance is like chaining yourself to negative emotions and expecting the other person to come and set you free. But the other person has probably also chained themselves to this and other negative emotions; thus, both of you are chained. If they cannot free themselves, how are they going to free you? You can only free yourself when you realize that it is you who can chain and unchain yourself.

It is true that, it is never what happened that matters but

instead it is how you react to what happened. What happened pales in comparison to how you respond. The power is all in you. When you respond angrily, hatefully, or with the perception of being a victim, then you are giving power to that action or person to hurt you. You become the slave of the situations, actions, and people. It will not be long before someone else also hurts you, angers you, or makes you their victim, hence owning your mind like a master owns a slave. You unconsciously become a slave that depends on circumstances or people to determine how good or bad your day should be.

Let's say someone hurts your feelings or betrays you. Then why do you more than double the hurt by having negative thoughts like anger, hate, or feelings of victimization? Your own response hurts you far more than the actions of others. Whatever negative or bad thoughts you have are hurting you but not the other person. Be smart and stop hurting yourself.

Can you imagine? All that fear, rage, stress, and victimhood—you brought upon yourself. Even though there were different perpetrators of these experiences, ultimately it was you who sowed the seed through your very thoughts and responses and then reaped what you sow. You can blame people and circumstances, but ultimately you are the only one who has the power to allow these things to become your reality.

You can choose to allow anger to enslave your mind and waste your life by letting it waste your time, creativity, energy, and peace or by letting it put you in jail for murder or hurting someone. You can also choose to become a master by using anger to enlighten you, to teach you more about yourself, to make you more creative, to learn about others, to inspire others, to learn how to maintain peace and teach yourself how to forgive. Your choice determines whether you are a free person or a slave. See anger as a blessing to acquire wisdom rather than seeing anger as a curse that came to waste your life. You can use a knife to cook for yourself and someone, or you can use a knife to hurt yourself or hurt someone.

No One Can Hurt the Sage

No one can hurt the sage. Use every circumstance for your benefit.
Be the alchemist who transmutes the dark energy into light.
Stop the illusions of anger and hate
That are filling your mind with imaginary fights.

Give love and peace to your brothers and sisters,
And you will be blessed with more peace and happiness.
For what you give is what you receive in the end.
Use each day as a chance to get one more loving friend.

Printed in the United States
By Bookmasters